NATIONAL ACADEMIES
Sciences
Engineering
Medicine

NATIONAL ACADEMIES PRESS
Washington, DC

Law Enforcement Use of Probabilistic Genotyping, Forensic DNA Phenotyping, and Forensic Investigative Genetic Genealogy Technologies

Erin Hammers Forstag, *Rapporteur*

Committee on Law and Justice

Computer Science and Telecommunications Board

Division of Behavioral and Social Sciences and Education

Division on Engineering and Physical Sciences

Proceedings of a Workshop

NATIONAL ACADEMIES PRESS 500 Fifth Street, NW Washington, DC 20001

This activity was supported by a contract between the National Academy of Sciences and the National Institute of Justice (15PNIJ-23-GG-04263-NIJB). Any opinions, findings, conclusions, or recommendations expressed in this publication do not necessarily reflect the views of any organization or agency that provided support for the project.

International Standard Book Number-13: 978-0-309-72364-0
International Standard Book Number-10: 0-309-72364-7
Digital Object Identifier: https://doi.org/10.17226/27887

This publication is available from the National Academies Press, 500 Fifth Street, NW, Keck 360, Washington, DC 20001; (800) 624-6242; http://www.nap.edu.

Copyright 2024 by the National Academy of Sciences. National Academies of Sciences, Engineering, and Medicine and National Academies Press and the graphical logos for each are all trademarks of the National Academy of Sciences. All rights reserved.

Printed in the United States of America.

Suggested citation: National Academies of Sciences, Engineering, and Medicine. 2024. *Law Enforcement Use of Probabilistic Genotyping, Forensic DNA Phenotyping, and Forensic Investigative Genetic Genealogy Technologies: Proceedings of a Workshop*. Washington, DC: National Academies Press. https://doi.org/10.17226/27887.

The **National Academy of Sciences** was established in 1863 by an Act of Congress, signed by President Lincoln, as a private, nongovernmental institution to advise the nation on issues related to science and technology. Members are elected by their peers for outstanding contributions to research. Dr. Marcia McNutt is president.

The **National Academy of Engineering** was established in 1964 under the charter of the National Academy of Sciences to bring the practices of engineering to advising the nation. Members are elected by their peers for extraordinary contributions to engineering. Dr. John L. Anderson is president.

The **National Academy of Medicine** (formerly the Institute of Medicine) was established in 1970 under the charter of the National Academy of Sciences to advise the nation on medical and health issues. Members are elected by their peers for distinguished contributions to medicine and health. Dr. Victor J. Dzau is president.

The three Academies work together as the **National Academies of Sciences, Engineering, and Medicine** to provide independent, objective analysis and advice to the nation and conduct other activities to solve complex problems and inform public policy decisions. The National Academies also encourage education and research, recognize outstanding contributions to knowledge, and increase public understanding in matters of science, engineering, and medicine.

Learn more about the National Academies of Sciences, Engineering, and Medicine at **www.nationalacademies.org**.

Consensus Study Reports published by the National Academies of Sciences, Engineering, and Medicine document the evidence-based consensus on the study's statement of task by an authoring committee of experts. Reports typically include findings, conclusions, and recommendations based on information gathered by the committee and the committee's deliberations. Each report has been subjected to a rigorous and independent peer-review process and it represents the position of the National Academies on the statement of task.

Proceedings published by the National Academies of Sciences, Engineering, and Medicine chronicle the presentations and discussions at a workshop, symposium, or other event convened by the National Academies. The statements and opinions contained in proceedings are those of the participants and are not endorsed by other participants, the planning committee, or the National Academies.

Rapid Expert Consultations published by the National Academies of Sciences, Engineering, and Medicine are authored by subject-matter experts on narrowly focused topics that can be supported by a body of evidence. The discussions contained in rapid expert consultations are considered those of the authors and do not contain policy recommendations. Rapid expert consultations are reviewed by the institution before release.

For information about other products and activities of the National Academies, please visit www.nationalacademies.org/about/whatwedo.

WORKSHOP PLANNING COMMITTEE ON LAW ENFORCEMENT USE OF PROBABILISTIC GENOTYPING, FORENSIC DNA PHENOTYPING, AND FORENSIC INVESTIGATIVE GENETIC GENEALOGY TECHNOLOGIES

ALICIA CARRIQUIRY (*Chair*), Professor of Statistics, Iowa State University
SARAH CHU, Director of Policy and Reforms, Perlmutter Center for Legal Justice at Cardozo Law
MICHAEL COBLE, Associate Professor and Executive Director, Center for Human Identification at the University of North Texas Health Science Center
HEATHER McKIERNAN, Forensic Services Program Manager for the National Missing and Unidentified Persons System, RTI International
CRAIG O'CONNOR, Deputy Director, Forensic Biology Department of the New York City Office of Chief Medical Examiner
NATALIE RAM, Professor of Law, University of Maryland Francis King Carey School of Law; Adjunct Faculty, Berman Institute of Bioethics at Johns Hopkins University

Staff

AMANDA GRIGG, Senior Program Officer
ABIGAIL ALLEN, Associate Program Officer
STACEY SMIT, Program Coordinator
EMILY P. BACKES, Deputy Board Director

Acknowledgments

The National Academies of Sciences, Engineering, and Medicine's Committee on Law and Justice (CLAJ) wishes to express its sincere gratitude to the planning committee chair, Alicia Carriquiry, for her valuable contributions to the development and orchestration of this workshop. CLAJ also wishes to thank all the members of the planning committee, who collaborated to ensure the workshop included an abundance of informative presentations and moderated discussions. CLAJ would also like to recognize the critical support of our workshop sponsor, the National Institute of Justice, without which we could not have undertaken this project. It is due to that organization's dedication to improving knowledge and understanding of crime and justice issues through science that we were able to facilitate this timely event.

Reviewers

This Proceedings of a Workshop was reviewed in draft form by individuals chosen for their diverse perspectives and technical expertise. The purpose of this independent review is to provide candid and critical comments that will assist the National Academies of Sciences, Engineering, and Medicine (National Academies) in making each published proceedings as sound as possible and to ensure that it meets the institutional standards for quality, objectivity, evidence, and responsiveness to the charge. The review comments and draft manuscript remain confidential to protect the integrity of the process.

We thank the following individuals for their review of this proceedings:

JOHN M. BUTLER, National Institute of Standards and Technology
DAPHNE OLUWASEUN MARTSCHENKO, Stanford Center for Biomedical Ethics

We also thank staff member **STEPHEN F. MAHER** for reading and providing helpful comments on this manuscript.

Although the reviewers listed above provided many constructive comments and suggestions, they were not asked to endorse the content of the proceedings nor did they see the final draft before its release. The review of this proceedings was overseen by **ALEX PIQUERO,** University of Miami. He was responsible for making certain that an independent examination of this proceedings was carried out in accordance with standards of the National Academies and that all review comments were carefully considered. Responsibility for the final content rests entirely with the rapporteur and the National Academies.

Contents

Acronyms and Abbreviations   xvii

1   Public Trust and the Landscape of Law Enforcement Use of Advanced Forensic DNA Technologies   1
ORGANIZATION OF THE PROCEEDINGS, 1
OPENING REMARKS, 4
SETTING THE STAGE: ETHICS, EQUITY, AND ACCOUNTABILITY, 5
    Context and Framing, 5
    Expanded Impact of Advanced Forensic DNA Technologies Context and Framing, 7
    Law Enforcement Use of Proprietary Technologies, 7
    Accuracy and Transparence, 8
    Regulation and Oversight, 9
    Indigenous Communities, 11
    Downstream Implications, 11
    Public Understanding, 12
    Ethical and Socially Responsible Implementation, 14
SURVEYING THE LANDSCAPE, 15
    Scope of Use, 15
    Opportunities and Benefits, 16
    Technology's Role in Investigative Work, 18
    Challenges and Ethical Considerations, 18
    Audience Questions, 20

2   **Forensic Investigative Genetic Genealogy**   23
    OVERVIEW OF FORENSIC INVESTIGATIVE GENETIC
       GENEALOGY (FIGG), 23
       Process of FIGG, 25
       Distinct Characteristics of FIGG, 26
       Public Perspectives on FIGG, 28
    CONSIDERATIONS FOR USE OF FIGG BY LAW
       ENFORCEMENT, 30
       Opportunities, 30
       Challenges and Ethical Considerations, 32
       Considerations for Implementation, 34
    REFLECTIONS, 39

3   **Probabilistic Genotyping**   41
    OVERVIEW OF PG, 41
    CONSIDERATIONS FOR PG USE BY LAW
       ENFORCEMENT, 45
       Opportunities, 45
       Challenges and Ethical Considerations, 46
       Considerations for Implementation, 50
    REFLECTIONS, 52

4   **Forensic DNA Phenotyping**   55
    OVERVIEW OF FORENSIC DNA PHENOTYPING (FDP), 55
    CONSIDERATIONS FOR FDP USE BY LAW
       ENFORCEMENT, 58
       Opportunities, 58
       Challenges and Ethical Considerations, 61
    CONSIDERATIONS FOR IMPLEMENTATION, 63
       Ethical Considerations, 63
       Frameworks for Governance and Oversight, 64
    REFLECTIONS, 65

5   **Learning from Abroad**   67
    BEST PRACTICES AMID A REGULATORY VACUUM
       IN AUSTRALIA, 67
    TENTATIVE USE OF FIGG IN EUROPE, 71
    A LACK OF CLARITY IN ENGLAND AND WALES, 72
    MULTIPLE LEVELS OF REGULATION IN
       SWITZERLAND, 74
    GENERAL DATA PROTECTION REGULATION, 75
    BLIND TESTING, 75

6	Moving Forward: Priorities for Research and Funding	77
	HIGH-PRIORITY ACTIONABLE ISSUES, 77	
	Disparate Impacts of Technology, 78	
	Reliability, 79	
	Funding as Leverage, 79	
	Existing Frameworks, 79	
	Federal Research Priorities, 80	
	Cross-Discipline Collaboration, 81	
	Regulation and Oversight, 82	
	CLOSING REFLECTIONS, 84	
	Education and Training, 84	
	Culture of Science, 84	
	Regulation and Oversight, 85	
	Formal Systems of Repair, 86	
	Next Steps, 86	

References   89

Appendixes

A	Public Meeting Agendas	93
B	Workshop Planning Committee and Speaker Biographies	97
C	Bibliography for Workshop Speaker Presentations	111

Boxes, Figures, and Table

BOXES

1-1   Executive Order 14074, 2
1-2   Statement of Task, 3
1-3   Brief Technology Definitions, 4
1-4   Regulations and Guidance on Law Enforcement Use of Non–Law Enforcement Genetic Genealogy Databases, 10

2-1   Overview of Forensic Investigative Genetic Genealogy, 24
2-2   Opportunities and Challenges in Using FIGG Identified by Workshop Speakers, 31
2-3   Guidelines for Establishing FIGG Programs, 35
2-4   Maryland Code, Criminal Procedure § 17-102, 36

3-1   Overview of Probabilistic Genotyping and Related Software, 42
3-2   SWGDAM Guidelines for Validating Probabilistic Genotyping Systems, 44
3-3   Opportunities and Challenges in Using PG Identified by Workshop Speakers, 46
3-4   IEEE Standard 1012 for System, Software, and Hardware Verification and Validation, 50

4-1   Overview of Forensic DNA Phenotyping, 56
4-2   Opportunities and Challenges in Using FDP Identified by Workshop Speakers, 60

5-1   Best Practices for Privacy Impact Assessments, 69
5-2   Australian Regulations on FIGG, 70

6-1   Further Reading, 83

FIGURES

2-1   U.S. general population survey of support for forensic investigative genetic genealogy: 2018, 29
2-2   Nine priority issues for FIGG as identified by policy Delphi, 30

3-1   Implementation of probabilistic genotyping, 2014–2023, 45

4-1   Examples of forensic DNA phenotyping (FDP) prediction result using current scientific knowledge, 59
4-2   Reliability, utility, and legitimacy framework for the ethical implementation of forensic DNA phenotyping, 64

5-1   Sequential unmasking of information before using forensic investigative genetic genealogy (FIGG), 71

TABLE

2-1   Differences Between Traditional Forensic DNA Analysis and Genetic Genealogy, 27

Acronyms and Abbreviations

AUC   area under the curve

BGA   inference of biographical ancestry

CODIS   Combined DNA Index System

DNA   deoxyribonucleic acid
DOJ   U.S. Department of Justice

ELSI   ethical, legal, and social implications

FDP   forensic DNA phenotyping
FIGG   forensic investigative genetic genealogy

GDPR   General Data Protection Regulation

I-FAMILIA   INTERPOL Family Associated Matching to Identify Lost Individuals Abroad
IEEE   Institute of Electrical and Electronics Engineers
INTERPOL   International Criminal Police Organization

NCIDD   National Criminal Identification DNA Database
NIJ   National Institute of Justice
NTVIC   National Technology Validation and Implementation Collaborative

PG	probabilistic genotyping
SNP	single nucleotide polymorphism
STR	short tandem repeat
SWGDAM	Scientific Working Group on DNA Analysis Methods
Y-STR	Y-chromosome short tandem repeat

1

Public Trust and the Landscape of Law Enforcement Use of Advanced Forensic DNA Technologies

To better understand key considerations around law enforcement use of advanced forensic DNA technologies, the Committee on Law and Justice and the Computer Science and Telecommunications Board at the National Academies of Sciences, Engineering, and Medicine (National Academies) held a workshop titled "Law Enforcement Use of Probabilistic Genotyping, Forensic DNA Phenotyping, and Forensic Investigative Genetic Genealogy Technologies." The workshop was organized in response to Executive Order 14074 (Box 1-1), issued in May 2022, and was held on March 13 and 14, 2024. The order focused on advancing effective, accountable policing, as well as criminal justice practices around algorithmic approaches to policing; it directed the National Academies to hold a workshop to explore the different approaches. The workshop, organized according to a statement of task (Box 1-2) and sponsored by the National Institute of Justice, focused on three specific advanced forensic DNA practices: probabilistic genotyping, forensic DNA phenotyping, and forensic investigative genetic genealogy (see Box 1-3 for working definitions of these terms).[1]

ORGANIZATION OF THE PROCEEDINGS

This proceedings describes the workshop panel presentations and the discussion that followed each panel. The chapters are organized around

---

[1] Where possible, this proceedings refers specifically to forensic DNA technologies by name (e.g., probabilistic genotyping). At times, the three technologies in focus in this workshop are referred to more broadly as "advanced forensic DNA technologies."

> **BOX 1-1**
> **Executive Order 14074**
>
> On May 25, 2022, President Joe Biden issued the Executive Order on Advancing Effective, Accountable Policing and Criminal Justice Practices to Enhance Public Trust and Public Safety. The order highlights issues of core public concern, including imperatives to "live up to our principles as a Nation," and "to build secure, safe, and healthy communities" (Exec. Order No. 14,074 § 1). The order specifically centers the importance of trust between law enforcement and the communities it serves and states that public trust requires that the criminal legal system embody "fair and equal treatment, transparency, and accountability" (Exec. Order No. 14,074 § 1). Noting that the bonds of trust have been frayed or broken in some communities in America—particularly in Black and Brown communities—the order acknowledges the legacy of systemic racism in the criminal justice system and calls for Americans to work together to eliminate enduring racial disparities. This work includes taking proactive measures to prevent profiling based on race, ethnicity, national origin, and other characteristics; ensuring that new law enforcement technologies do not exacerbate disparities; and increasing transparency by collecting data and making it available to the public.
>
> The executive order issues a broad range of directives aimed at addressing these issues of public concern, on topics including law enforcement officer recruitment and training, standards for use of force, responding to individuals in mental health crises, and alternatives to incarceration. Among these directives is a requirement that the attorney general call on the National Academy of Sciences to conduct a study of technologies and algorithms used by law enforcement, including facial recognition technology, other technologies using biometric information, and predictive algorithms. In particular, the executive order asks the National Academy of Sciences to focus on identifying any privacy, civil rights, civil liberties, accuracy, or disparate impact concerns raised by law enforcement use of these tools.
>
> SOURCE: Exec. Order No. 14,074, 2022.

the key topics of the workshop, with some chapters including summaries of related content from multiple panels. Chapter 1 introduces these key technologies and gives an overview of their use in law enforcement, and discusses the ethics, equity, and accountability issues that have emerged as the technologies are being implemented. Chapters 2, 3, and 4 each focus on a specific technology and explore the unique aspects of the technology, the related risks and ethical issues, and considerations for implementation. Chapter 2 focuses on forensic investigative genetic genealogy, Chapter 3 focuses on probabilistic genotyping, and Chapter 4 focuses on forensic DNA phenotyping. Chapter 5 looks at forensic DNA technologies from a global perspective, exploring their use in Australia, Europe, the United Kingdom,

> **BOX 1-2**
> **Statement of Task**
>
> The National Academies will convene a planning committee to conduct a two-day public workshop on law enforcement use of probabilistic genotyping, forensic DNA phenotyping, and forensic investigative genetic genealogy technologies. It will explore the following:
>
> - How are probabilistic genotyping, facial predictions, and genetic genealogy being used by law enforcement across federal, state, local, tribal, and territorial actors?
> - How reliable and accurate are these methods in practice?
> - What are the relevant legal considerations and precedents that accompany these new technologies?
> - What are the disparate impact concerns raised by these technologies or their manner of use?
> - What considerations (e.g., accuracy of these technologies, including underlying issues of sensitivity and specificity; privacy, civil rights, civil liberties; and disparate impact) need to be assessed in implementing these technologies and the use of genetic material by law enforcement?
> - What are institutional considerations for operations and procedures to ensure that these technologies are being used effectively and equitably?
>
> The workshop was designed to explore the issues articulated in the statement of task. Presentations and discussions focused primarily on the evolving use of advanced forensic DNA technologies in law enforcement, with a specific focus on probabilistic genotyping, forensic DNA phenotyping, and forensic investigative genetic genealogy.

and Switzerland. Finally, Chapter 6 summarizes workshop discussions on research gaps and funding needs for emerging forensic DNA technologies and describes the key themes of the workshop as identified by individual speakers.

The full meeting agenda and biographical sketches of planning committee members and workshop presenters appear in Appendixes A and B, respectively. Appendix C provides a bibliography of resources mentioned by workshop speakers.

This proceedings has been prepared by the workshop rapporteur as a factual summary of what occurred at the workshop. The views contained in the proceedings are those of the individual workshop participants and do not necessarily represent the views of other workshop participants, the workshop planning committee, or the National Academies.

> **BOX 1-3**
> **Brief Technology Definitions**
>
> The following definitions reflect information shared in presentations from multiple workshop speakers. They should not be construed as consensus or exhaustive definitions of the topics discussed. For more detailed descriptions of each technology and its core processes, actors, and relevant regulations, see the Technology Overview Boxes that begin Chapters 2, 3, and 4.
>
> **Forensic investigative genetic genealogy** is a multistep, multidisciplinary process that combines advanced DNA analysis, genetic genealogy databases, and traditional genealogical methods to generate investigative leads and putative identities for previously unknown DNA samples.
>
> **Probabilistic genotyping software** is a forensic tool used to analyze and interpret complex DNA evidence from crime scenes (e.g., DNA samples that include multiple sources, are limited in quantity, and/or damaged). It employs advanced statistical modeling and computer algorithms to calculate the probability that a DNA sample matches a person of interest or an unknown individual. Probabilistic genotyping has two main functions: (a) mixture deconvolution to determine what genotypes could be contributors to a sample, and (b) calculation of the statistical weight of a comparison to a person of interest.
>
> **Forensic DNA phenotyping** is a technique that aims to predict visible physical characteristics and biogeographical ancestry of an unknown person from DNA evidence left at a crime scene, typically used for investigative lead generation. It is an investigative intelligence tool that provides information about likely physical traits of a person of interest from DNA to help inform or narrow a police investigation, rather than a means of definitive identification as in traditional DNA profiling.
>
> SOURCE: Definitions presented by Heather McKiernan and Craig O'Connor on March 13, 2024.

OPENING REMARKS

Alicia Carriquiry, Iowa State University and chair of the workshop planning committee, began the event with brief opening remarks. Carriquiry noted that the workshop was a direct response to Executive Order 14074 on advancing effective, accountable policing and criminal justice practices that enhance public trust and public safety (Exec. Order No. 14,074, 2022). She further noted that the executive order emphasizes the need to ensure public trust in law enforcement, and that the workshop would consider a range of considerations around implementation of advanced forensic genetic technologies, including risks associated with privacy, civil rights, and equity, which have the potential to erode public trust. Carriquiry recognized the planning committee, a multidisciplinary group of experts convened by the National Academies, who collaborated to develop the workshop agenda and select speakers.

Following these remarks, Lucas Zarwell, National Institute of Justice (NIJ), provided additional context for the workshop, stating that NIJ has been involved in forensic science for 50 years, with the mission of supporting state, local, and tribal advancements through the development of new technologies and the dissemination of best practices. NIJ utilizes a "listen, learn, and inform" approach and places great value in the collaborative spaces that the National Academies creates. Zarwell explained that the 2015 National Academies report *Support for Forensic Science Research* is still used by NIJ to guide its actions and strategic planning. The theme at the American Academy of Forensic Sciences meeting this year, noted Zarwell, was "Justice for All." Workshops like this, he said, are necessary for exploring the power of new technologies while also considering how they can be used to ensure justice for all.

SETTING THE STAGE: ETHICS, EQUITY, AND ACCOUNTABILITY

Following brief introductory remarks by members of the workshop planning committee, the event began with a panel highlighting the topics of public concern at the center of the executive order that motivated the workshop. Speakers discussed issues of ethics, equity, and accountability related to the use of advanced forensic DNA technologies by law enforcement. Five panelists with expertise in civil and human rights, privacy, civil liberties law, biomedical ethics, public health, and community research offered remarks on these topics, with moderation by Sarah Chu, Perlmutter Center for Legal Justice at Cardozo Law.

Context and Framing

Chu opened the workshop by emphasizing the importance of discussing ethics, equity, and accountability in the context of law enforcement's use of technologies like probabilistic genotyping, forensic DNA phenotyping, and forensic investigative genetic genealogy. She began the discussion by asking panelists what issues they viewed as central to considerations of law enforcement use of advanced forensic DNA technologies. Tierra Bradford, Leadership Conference on Civil Rights, pointed to historical and ongoing disparities in the criminal legal system and the potential for new tools to exacerbate or entrench them. She explained that she approached this discussion with a focus on civil rights, stating that the criminal legal system, as it currently exists, is unfair and inequitable. Bradford then expressed concern that the introduction of new technologies, if not properly verified, validated, and implemented, could exacerbate these inequalities. Furthermore, she pointed to the need to address the recurring issues of transparency and accountability, public understanding of and engagement with the criminal legal system, and the complexity of private, for-profit vendors serving public institutions.

Jennifer Lynch, Electronic Frontier Foundation, explained that she approached the workshop through the lens of privacy and surveillance. Top of mind for her, she explained, was the extent to which advanced forensic genetic technologies could implicate those outside of the criminal legal system, including close relatives of suspects (in the case of forensic investigative genetic genealogy), and even the broader public (in the cases of forensic investigative genetic genealogy and forensic DNA phenotyping). Regarding forensic DNA phenotyping, Lynch noted that disseminating an image to the public of an individual suspected of perpetrating a crime has risks. For example, an image of a Black suspect could implicate an innocent member of the Black community, particularly given known challenges with eyewitness and cross-race identification. Lynch provided an example of these risks in practice, pointing to a recent case with the Edmonton Police Service in Canada. She suggested that law enforcement use of advanced forensic DNA technologies represents a significant change in how DNA is utilized for criminal investigations, because of its expanded scope of impact, and the implementation of the underlying science to law enforcement practice poses significant questions.

Drawing on her expertise in bioethics, Daphne Martschenko, Stanford University, stressed the importance of considering the ethical and social implications of genomic research and the need to include diverse voices in these discussions. Martschenko outlined her focus on the ethical, legal, and social implications of human genetic and genomic technologies; on innovations to expand the communities included in weighing risks and benefits of genomic research; and on the development of harm mitigation and benefit promotion strategies, each of which are necessary for responsible use of the technologies at the center of the workshop. She emphasized the necessity of grounding conversations about the use of advanced forensic DNA technologies in ethical and social considerations.

Finally, Krystal Tsosie, Arizona State University, introduced herself as a citizen of the Navajo Nation and an Indigenous geneticist-bioethicist, with expertise in Indigenous genomic data sovereignty.[2] She explained that her work is characterized by a strong commitment to ethical practices, Indigenous community engagement, and data sovereignty, and that this work directly intersects with law enforcement use of advanced forensic DNA technologies to identify missing or murdered Indigenous persons. Tsosie shared how Indigenous peoples and communities have sometimes been

---

[2] Indigenous genomic data sovereignty involves the right of Indigenous peoples to have agency and authority over DNA collection from their nations.

pressured to contribute their genetic information to databases to identify victims and rematriate[3] their remains to their families and communities and reflected on how such pressures could be applied around use of technologies like forensic investigative genetic genealogy.

Expanded Impact of Advanced Forensic DNA Technologies Context and Framing

Lynch directed attention to the differences between advanced forensic DNA technologies and more traditional forensic approaches to DNA analysis and discussed the broader public implications of adopting new DNA technologies. In addition to the potential expanded scope of impact, she suggested that such tools represent a major shift from the previous system of comparing DNA from a crime scene with a database of convicted felons. Now, Lynch said, criminal investigations have the potential to implicate not just people directly involved in the criminal legal system, but extended family members, and even the broader public. Members of the public are involved when their genetic information from genealogy databases is used in a criminal investigation, or when a computer-generated image is released and might implicate members of an entire racial community. This expanded scope of impact, Lynch suggested, means that forensic investigative genetic genealogy and forensic DNA phenotyping represent a significant change from previous uses of DNA in the criminal legal system. She emphasized the importance of considering advanced forensic DNA technologies through the lens of their impact on individuals, communities, and privacy interests.

Law Enforcement Use of Proprietary Technologies

Central to the discussion was a recognition by the speakers of the role of private industry in the development and sale of genetic technologies for use by public institutions—in this case, law enforcement. Ethics in industry operates in a unique space, said Tsosie, as compared to the highly regulated areas of academic research and clinical practice. She outlined how companies involved in developing, marketing, and distributing advanced forensic DNA technologies acquire DNA as an asset, with databases and companies being bought and sold frequently. The question, she asked, is what is happening to the informed consent and the terms of use to which individuals

---

[3] *Rematriation* is a holistic movement led by Indigenous women, focused on the revitalization of Indigenous cultures, knowledge systems, and sacred feminine relationships with lands and waters as a means of decolonization, healing, and restoration of balance (Sogorea Te' Land Trust, 2021). Tsosie also qualified rematriation as a shift in power dynamics as it relates to data ownership, sharing that it is more restorative in equity than other approaches.

who contributed their DNA originally agreed? She expressed concern about the possibility that original privacy policies may not be honored by the new owner and that databases could become "open for mining" by other entities and uses to which contributors did not consent. Tsosie explained how this potential "data co-option" raises ethical and jurisdictional concerns, particularly for historically marginalized communities.

Lynch spoke to the reality that private companies are heavily involved in forensic sciences. Based on her professional experience, she described the difficulty of auditing the work of these companies, in part because of the complexity of the technology and in part because the source code and external verification and validation studies may not be readily available. This puts defendants at a disadvantage, remarked Lynch. She explained that while some defendants have gained access to the source code, they have obtained this information by hiring their own experts and agreeing to protective orders. She explained that information they uncover about the validity or accuracy of the technologies typically remains under protective order, so future defendants cannot access the information for their own defenses. Lynch emphasized that trade secrets protections for private companies also complicate the use of forensic investigative genetic genealogy and forensic DNA phenotyping by justice system actors because the data and the algorithms that companies use to analyze DNA are not readily available for the public or defendants to examine, or for independent validation or peer review. Bradford expressed her perception of the incongruity between a lack of transparency and the possibility that such information can have a substantial impact (in the form of state power) on individuals and communities.

Accuracy and Transparency

Bradford emphasized the significant negative impact that engagement with the criminal legal system can have on individuals and communities. Even a few days spent in jail can result in the loss of housing, employment, and/or custody of children. She indicated that transparency, accuracy, and accountability of advanced forensic DNA technologies are essential when weighed against the potential for negative impacts to individuals and downstream impacts on their communities. Bradford called for adequate training and education, risk management, continued monitoring, evaluations, and regulations around advanced forensic DNA technologies. She also stated that if these measures indicate that advanced forensic DNA technologies are found to have disparate impact, they should not continue to be used by law enforcement.

Advanced forensic DNA technologies are used to try to solve crimes that are "heinous" and may be associated with families who have been seeking justice for a long time, said Lynch. She further noted that without transparency, oversight, and ongoing evaluation of law enforcement use of forensic DNA phenotyping, its use could lead to the implication of innocent persons. She explained that this is a particular problem for any technologies making use of facial predictions in cross-race crimes, because individuals typically have a difficult time identifying people of a different race. Furthermore, in crimes where an eyewitness has a memory of the perpetrator, a computer-generated image can influence and even override an individual's original memory. This loss of the eyewitness perspective is a loss to the criminal investigation, she said.

Issues of accuracy and transparency lead to related concerns about the lack of standardization for advanced forensic DNA technologies, said Martschenko. She suggested that inconsistent or inadequate regulation of DNA samples leaves the door open for upstream and downstream misuse and abuse by actors in the criminal legal system, a fear born from real examples of scientific exploitation of historically marginalized populations. Martschenko argued that greater transparency can help to dispel the notion that genetic technologies are foolproof, objective, accurate, and without fault. She noted earlier the lack of incentives for researchers to consider downstream outcomes and called for mechanisms to ensure transparency and accountability in the use of all advanced forensic DNA technologies.

Regulation and Oversight

On the topics of privacy and consent, Lynch explained that she struggles with advising people to provide their DNA to any database, given that their information is most likely not explicitly protected by law, creating significant privacy concerns for users. Law enforcement can access non–law enforcement genetic genealogy databases via legal processes or under specific conditions, and Lynch noted that commercial genetic genealogy databases have effectively created a national, unregulated database that could enable identification of up to 95% of people in the United States with Western European ancestry. While no comprehensive federal regulations specifically govern the use of genetic genealogy databases by law enforcement, some states have enacted laws to regulate this practice and the U.S. Department of Justice (DOJ) has issued interim policies recommending the use of non–law enforcement genetic databases only for unsolved violent crimes where other methods have failed (Box 1-4). In contrast, said Lynch, criminal justice DNA databases (e.g., Combined DNA Index System[4]) have been the

---

[4] The Combined DNA Index System, or CODIS, is a computer software program that operates local, state, and national databases of DNA profiles from convicted offenders, unsolved crime scene evidence, and missing persons (Federal Bureau of Investigation, n.d.a).

subject of much public debate, and many regulations are in place to control access to the data. Lynch pointed to Maryland Criminal Procedure Code § 17-102 as a leading example of state efforts to govern the use of forensic investigative genetic genealogy in criminal investigations by addressing the misuse of genetic information (see Box 2-4 in Chapter 2). She noted that the law balances public safety interests with privacy rights by prohibiting unauthorized disclosure of genetic data, establishing criminal penalties for violations, and allowing civil damages for wrongful disclosures.

BOX 1-4
Regulations and Guidance on Law Enforcement Use of Non–Law Enforcement Genetic Genealogy Databases

Commercial Databases

Law enforcement can access genetic genealogy databases, but typically this requires a proper legal process, such as a search warrant or court order. For example, some companies require a valid court order, subpoena, or search warrant to allow access to their data. Some databases allow law enforcement access under specific conditions, such as for investigating violent crimes, and users can opt in or out of allowing their data to be used for these purposes.

State Laws

Maryland and Montana have recently enacted laws that regulate law enforcement's use of genetic genealogy databases for criminal investigations. These are the first state laws in the United States specifically regulating the use of forensic investigative genetic genealogy by law enforcement. The laws aim to balance the utility of this technique in solving violent crimes with protecting genetic privacy rights and preventing misuse. While some companies previously allowed law enforcement access with user consent enabled by default, these new laws impose stricter judicial oversight and consent requirements.

Federal Guidance

The U.S. Department of Justice (DOJ, 2019) issued an interim policy that provides guidance on the use of forensic genetic genealogy by law enforcement agencies. This policy outlines the conditions under which non–law enforcement genetic databases can be used to generate investigative leads for unsolved violent crimes. It provides a framework for law enforcement agencies to use genetic genealogy databases responsibly and ethically, while ensuring that this technique is reserved for the most serious and unresolved violent crime cases where other investigative methods have been exhausted. By recommending the use of non–law enforcement genetic databases only as a last resort for unsolved violent crimes, the DOJ's interim policy seeks to maintain public trust and address concerns about potential misuse or overreach in the application of this investigative technique.

SOURCE: Generated by the rapporteur based on workshop presentations from March 13 and 14, 2024.

Indigenous Communities

Turning to issues specifically impacting Indigenous people and communities, Tsosie explained that the rate of violence against Native populations and Indigenous people is several-fold higher than against other groups. "Genetics is a poor solution to violence," said Tsosie, quoting an X (formerly Twitter) post from the prominent bioinformatician Larry Hunter (2019). She suggested that law enforcement should focus resources on efforts to reduce race-based violence from being perpetuated onto Indigenous people, rather than seeking post hoc measures such as the expansion of genetic databases to identify perpetrators and victims. Advanced forensic DNA technologies present several unique risks for Indigenous communities, said Tsosie, and these risks are still being identified and navigated.

Tsosie questioned the meaning of *Indigenous* in the context of DNA, noting that there are 574 federally recognized tribes in the United States, as well as state-recognized or unrecognized tribes, and they all have distinct cultures, languages, demographics, genetic histories, and phenotypes. She stressed that there is a need to question how using DNA as a signifier of race and ethnicity fits in with this reality. Using DNA to identify race opens the door to racial genomic profiling, said Tsosie. She explained that due to the comparatively large size of families in Indigenous communities, one DNA test could implicate a huge portion of the community. Furthermore, relying on DNA technologies to solve crimes puts the onus on victims, their families, and their communities to contribute their genetic information. Many Indigenous families, said Tsosie, hear the message that, because Indigenous peoples are not well represented in genomic databases, it is their fault that their missing and murdered relatives cannot be identified, which can be a form of victim-blaming and coercion (Tsosie et al., 2021). She emphasized the importance of protecting tribal data and ensuring informed consent, stating that Indigenous communities need the opportunity to develop and control their own resources and policy frameworks in this space to determine whether these advanced forensic DNA technologies are beneficial rather than harmful to the community.

Downstream Implications

Martschenko noted that with new technologies, there is often a considerable gap between research that occurs upstream and the downstream use of the new tools. She explained that there are few incentives or mechanisms in academia to encourage researchers to consider the broader implications of their research or to include the voices of those who will be impacted in the research process. She emphasized that the benefits and risks of a new tool are often identified from the perspective of those creating the tool, rather than from the perspective of those who will be impacted. Marginalized communities have already been disproportionately harmed by the criminal justice system, said Martschenko, and advanced forensic DNA technologies have the potential to further these disparities. With emerging and evolving technologies, she said, it is often people who are already vulnerable who shoulder the potential harms.

A workshop audience member asked Martschenko to comment on how the concept of open science relates to the arena of genetic research. Martschenko acknowledged that there is a tension between the move toward open access, data sharing, and transparency, and the fact that studies can be used by actors with ill intent. For example, she explained how white supremacist groups have used social and behavioral genomics studies to justify violent, racist acts under the veneer of science. She said that there is a need to think deeply about the contexts in which data sharing may be appropriate and to what extent, and those in which sharing is not appropriate. For example, she explained that it may be inappropriate to share data collected via a years-long community engagement process with researchers who have no ties to the community and may want to use the data in ways that go against the values and goals of the community. Martschenko strongly encouraged researchers to think more critically about the context in which data are collected, for what purpose, and from whom, and to use this information to make decisions about when data sharing is appropriate. She also emphasized the value of implementing ethical frameworks for researchers that consider the social context of technology use.

Public Understanding

An audience member asked the panelists about the importance of educating the public on the uniqueness of genetic information and helping them to understand the implications of sharing their genetic information for various purposes. Tsosie answered that the public has a perception of DNA as being the "scientific arbiter of truth," partly because of its representation in popular culture and media. She emphasized the importance of communicating the limitations of advanced forensic DNA technologies, particularly in a courtroom setting, as a more realistic representation of the capabilities of the field. Bradford explained that in her professional capacity, she and her colleagues often "work backwards" to educate the public about a new topic. For example, when a person's civil rights are violated (e.g., they are wrongly incarcerated), she and her colleagues look back at what happened in the investigation and where mistakes were made, and then seek to understand the science behind the technologies that were involved in order to educate the public about the potential harms of certain technologies. She noted that this type of case-by-case approach is not ideal for large-scale education efforts, and that there is a need for scientists and advocates to work together to proactively educate the public on emerging technologies. Martschenko echoed Tsosie's emphasis on the importance of helping the public understand the limitations and ethical considerations of genomic technologies—namely, conveying the complexity of genetic information and moving away from the deterministic view of genetics. She then pointed to ongoing efforts to improve genetic literacy, which could be adapted and applied to a criminal legal context.

Martschenko provided two examples of organizations engaged in genetic literacy efforts. One such organization engaged in the promotion of genetic literacy is Personal Genetics Education & Dialogue, a nonprofit in Boston that creates curriculum for K–12 educators, holds public town halls, and partners with other groups to put on public-facing events on the ethical and social implications of genetics.[5] Additionally, the National Science Foundation has funded research aimed at overhauling high school biology curriculum in order to shift toward a more complex view of human genetic variation. Preliminary assessments of these approaches to genetic literacy, she said, have shown that teaching people about the probabilistic, complex nature of human variation has an effect on how they think about themselves and others and reduces genetic determinism and racial essentialism. Martschenko said that while this work is not specifically focused on the use of genetic information by law enforcement, a similar approach could be beneficial in helping the public better understand new technologies and their limitations.

Erin Murphy, New York University, added commentary as an audience member, suggesting that there is a "fundamental misapprehension" on the part of the public that the criminal legal system is monitoring and regulating the use of genetic information. The public assumes that there are scientific standards for admissible evidence, and that judges will be making decisions about the use of advanced forensic DNA technologies. However, she said, these technologies are used primarily in the investigative phase. Law enforcement does not need to disclose that they used genetic information to identify a suspect, or that they collected genetic information from a nontarget person in order to help the investigation. "There will be no constitutional motions" on these issues because they are not relevant to the actual criminal trial. The public may believe that the legal system has oversight of advanced forensic DNA technologies, she said, but in practice this is generally not true.

Martschenko emphasized that although even the experts do not yet have a full understanding of advanced forensic DNA technologies or a complete picture of how they are being used, they should not hesitate to

---

[5] For more information, see https://pged.org

bring the public into these conversations. It is important to be transparent about the uncertainty and lack of consensus among experts, and to allow the public to use their lived experiences to contribute to the conversation.

Ethical and Socially Responsible Implementation

Given all the challenges and risks associated with advanced forensic DNA technologies, said Chu, what would ethical implementation look like? Bradford said that it is critical to continually monitor and evaluate the use of the technologies and to not hesitate to put a ban or moratorium in place if necessary. For example, if assessments reveal that a technology has a disparate impact on a particular community, its use should be stopped. Martschenko added that while some technologies may eventually have benefits, using them while in their infancy presents greater risk of harm than benefit. If the tools are implemented while still untested, it can result in a situation where public mistrust is exacerbated, and the potential benefits of the tool do not get realized because of the damage already done. It is important to recognize the limited validity and utility of technologies and prevent them from being used inappropriately in high-stakes, life-or-death situations, she said.

Several speakers emphasized the need to think about public safety in the affirmative rather than focusing on solving crimes after they have occurred. Tsosie said that conversations and resources should be shifted toward preventing harm and violence in the first place. Bradford agreed and rhetorically asked what would happen if we invested more in health, education, violence intervention, and communities that are overpoliced.

Training of law enforcement and others using the technologies is key to ethical implementation, said Bradford, and agencies need to think about disparate impact and potential remedies, such as education and community-engaged participatory research. Communities that are most impacted—particularly communities of color—need to be brought into the conversation. These racialized groups are the "least considered [and] the most impacted," said Bradford. Martschenko added that in addition to impacted communities, a variety of other stakeholders need to be involved in conversations about the use of advanced forensic DNA technologies, including law enforcement, victims, industry, and the media. These groups need to be in dialogue about the risks and benefits of technologies and how to implement them in an ethical way. Martschenko emphasized that ethical implementation of these technologies requires a recognition of the social context in which they are implemented. Technologies do not operate in a vacuum; it is the responsibility of all stakeholders, from developers to law enforcement, to ensure that technologies are used appropriately and responsibly and do not cause further harm.

SURVEYING THE LANDSCAPE

The second workshop session featured perspectives of advanced forensic DNA technology users working within the criminal legal system. Panelists with professional experiences including criminal investigation, policing, forensic science, forensic laboratory management, and criminal prosecution engaged in moderated discussion about their day-to-day experiences with forensic DNA technologies and the challenges and opportunities they present. Craig O'Connor, New York City Office of Chief Medical Examiner, served as moderator.

Scope of Use

O'Connor began the discussion with the observation that probabilistic genotyping (PG) and forensic investigative genetic genealogy (FIGG) are more commonly used in law enforcement than forensic DNA phenotyping (FDP), and asked panelists about their own experiences with these technologies.

Speakers collectively identified PG as a dominant tool in forensic DNA analysis, widely adopted by more than 100 law enforcement and state laboratories in the United States. Leigh Clark, Florida Department of Law Enforcement, explained that PG helps forensic DNA analysts interpret DNA found at crime scenes—even when the DNA is limited in quantity, damaged, or mixed from different people—and then compare it with DNA from potential suspects.

Panelists identified FIGG as an emerging forensic technique that combines advanced DNA sequencing with traditional genealogical research to generate investigative leads. Paul Belli, International Homicide Investigators Association, said that FIGG has gained prominence for its role in solving high-profile cold cases, such as the identification of the Golden State Killer. He explained that FIGG has been instrumental in solving cases where other investigative methods have failed, providing new leads and revitalizing stagnant investigations.

Panelists described FDP as less commonly utilized by law enforcement, when compared with PG and FIGG. Belli and Clark both noted that their encounters with FDP were limited to a small number of cold cases. Belli emphasized that FDP use requires a thoughtful approach and an acknowledgment that the results are not definitive, but instead are investigative leads aimed at generating conversation around a case. Ensuring that communities do not perceive FDP results as a definitive picture of the subject, Belli noted, will require additional work by law enforcement. Clark agreed that FDP can potentially help generate investigative leads, particularly when there is no information about what the perpetrator looked like. She shared an example of a case where a behavioral profile suggested that the perpetrator was a middle-aged White man but phenotyping led the investigation in a different direction. Clark said that in contrast to Jennifer Lynch's experience, she has found vendors to be forthcoming about the capabilities and limitations of phenotyping products in their terms of service. She added that while phenotyping can be useful for some attributes—such as freckles, which is controlled by one gene—it cannot account for changes to people over time (e.g., weight). She indicated that FDP may have use in unidentified human remains cases where only anthropology has been used to discern outward physical characteristics associated with race or ethnicity.

Opportunities and Benefits

Unsolved Cases and Victim Services

Ray Valerio, Queens District Attorney's Office, opened the discussion of benefits with a reminder of the thousands of unsolved murders and sexual assault cases around the country. Thousands of victims, families, and communities are impacted by these cases, he said, and law enforcement has a duty to help solve these crimes. Valerio suggested that tools like PG and FIGG are invaluable in solving the most egregious crimes, including those committed against victims from historically marginalized communities, noting that in New York City, most violent crime victims are people of color. Mark Pooley, University of North Texas Center for Human Identification, noted that hundreds of unidentified human remains across the country have not been tested, representing a tragedy for families that do not know what happened to their loved ones. He posed that some families may never learn what happened to their loved ones unless advanced forensic genetic tools are used in their cases.

On the topic of unsolved cases, Pooley emphasized the pressure placed on detectives to solve cases. He offered a firsthand account of the experience of working on an unsolved homicide:

> It is one of the most frustrating things that's continually on your mind. And you're thinking, what else can I do? Because not only do you have to represent your department well, but you have to go to the families. And you tell them what you've done [to solve the case], if you've done very little, it's a slap in the face to the victim.

Pooley indicated that families appreciate knowing that detectives have used every tool at their disposal. On this note, Clark encouraged stakeholders to take a victim-centered approach to the implementation of advanced forensic genetic technologies.

Investigative Advantages

Another key benefit of advanced forensic DNA technologies, said Jeremy Triplett, Kentucky State Police Central Forensic Laboratory, is that they can provide more meaningful information than previous methods. For example, conducting probabilistic genotyping on a complex DNA mixture can help to exclude and include people from a sample that was previously uninterpretable. O'Connor explained that as forensic DNA technologies such as PG advance, forensic professionals can learn valuable investigative information from samples that were once too small or too low quality to interpret. Clark agreed that tools such as PG have provided significant enhancement to law enforcement's investigative capacity. She explained that PG has proven particularly effective in allowing DNA results to be used and interpreted in criminal cases, for inclusion and exclusion purposes, including in cold cases and postconviction exoneration.

Valerio spoke to this benefit from the perspective of attorneys. To illustrate, he shared that since 2010, guidelines from the Scientific Working Group on DNA Analysis Methods have required that any positive DNA match—where the DNA evidence links a suspect to a crime—must include a statistical measure. He noted that this is also mandated by the Federal Bureau of Investigation's Quality Assurance Standards. Valero remarked that this means when DNA evidence is presented in court, it must come with a statistical analysis that shows how likely it is that the DNA match is accurate. He said that including these statistics is crucial because it helps juries understand the strength of the DNA evidence presented and can help them evaluate all the evidence in the case and decide whether the suspect is guilty beyond a reasonable doubt.

Increased Accuracy and Reliability

In addition, the use of PG has improved the consistency of complex mixture interpretation. Triplett said that while PG results may differ depending on certain variables, the likelihood ratios generated within a laboratory are likely to be quite similar regardless of who is doing the work. He noted that the National Institute of Standards and Technology's Organization of Scientific Area Committees for Forensic Science Registry (2018) has a standard for validating PG systems and that a standard for assigning propositions to likelihood ratios is being developed (Academy Standards Board, 2021). These standards will bring more consistency in PG results both within and between labs, Triplett said. Clark said that discussions around PG often overcomplicate the technology. She argued that PG "doesn't really do anything that we weren't already doing" with prior DNA mixture interpretation approaches; it simply does it quicker and better than previous methods and considers multiple variables simultaneously. Laboratories conduct internal validation with their own known source data to ensure that the software functions correctly, she explained. Clark said that PG makes the interpretation within the laboratory more consistent from person to person, and it conducts the analysis without mathematical error and introduces much less subjectivity when statistical weight is calculated.

Technology's Role in Investigative Work

Pooley outlined the practical reality that advanced forensic DNA technologies do not replace traditional investigative work but supplement it. Law enforcement must still "put in the [investigative] work," but the information gleaned from advanced forensic DNA technologies can help point the investigation in a certain direction or provide new leads in a cold case. Belli concurred and said that advanced forensic DNA technologies are not used in a vacuum. Investigators do the work to get to the point of using one of the advanced forensic DNA technologies, and they use the information to continue the investigation. For example, the Golden State Killer case involved years of investigation, hundreds of interviews, and inclusion and exclusion of suspects before the case was ultimately cracked using FIGG. Valerio added that DNA is rarely the sole piece of evidence in a case, and forensic DNA technologies simply add information to the totality of the evidence for the jury to consider.

Clark said that the public sometimes mistakenly views forensic science as a silver bullet. Advanced forensic DNA technologies are enabling better utilization of the evidence that is collected, she said, but they are not magic. In order to make effective use of PG, for example, Clark explained that genetic material needs to be present in sufficient amounts at the crime scene, and the material then needs to be carefully collected and transported to the laboratory and analyzed. She emphasized that none of these steps operate independently of one another, explaining that each must be carried out successfully for PG to be utilized. While the integration of these technologies into investigative workflows has led to significant advancements in helping identify possible suspects, Clark suggested that there is room for additional education and training to improve law enforcement and lab execution of these processes from start to finish.

Challenges and Ethical Considerations

Regulation and Oversight

One challenge in the use of advanced forensic DNA technologies, said Belli, is inconsistent or lacking regulations among different jurisdictions.

As new technologies emerge, he said, it can be the "Wild West" until regulations catch up with practice. Belli noted that the conversations at this workshop, and the multiple perspectives represented, are critical to moving law enforcement use of advanced forensic DNA technologies forward in a thoughtful way. There is a need to find the middle ground between two distinct sides when considering the regulation of a new technology, said Dan Katz, Maryland State Police Forensic Sciences Division, describing his involvement with FIGG regulation in Maryland. Katz explained that in 2019, a bill was introduced to ban the practice of FIGG in the state. After this bill failed, relevant parties on both sides attempted to educate legislators about the issue, and progress was made but no bills were passed. In the third year, said Katz, the stakeholders came together to form a working group to find middle ground. Both sides conceded elements of what they wanted, he said, but everyone was relatively satisfied with the final regulations. Katz shared that his experiences working on Maryland Criminal Procedure Code § 17-102 have given him hope that relevant parties can collaborate productively as new technologies emerge.

In addition to legislation, several groups are working on best practices and guidelines for advanced forensic DNA technologies, said Valerio. The DOJ (2019) published an interim policy on FIGG in 2019 that lays out the requirements for the use of FIGG by law enforcement. The National Technology Validation and Implementation Collaborative has brought together stakeholders to develop guidelines and programs for new technologies; they recently published a guideline for FIGG programs in *Forensic Science International: Synergy* (Wickenheiser et al., 2023; see also Box 2-1 in Chapter 2). Courts are also weighing in on the appropriate use of advanced forensic DNA technologies, Valerio said. PG has been the subject of numerous evidentiary hearings across the country, and this process is building legal standards for the use of advanced forensic DNA technologies.

Using Results at Trial

Advanced forensic DNA technologies can also present unique challenges for attorneys attempting to address findings in legal proceedings, said Valerio. For example, he noted that it can be difficult to convey the statistical significance of the information provided by PG. Valerio suggested that lawyers are not generally comfortable with statistics, a subject area that is not taught in law school and does not appear on licensing exams or in continuing legal education courses. Despite these challenges, Valerio explained that prosecutors are responsible for presenting information in a way that appropriately upholds the scientific conclusions and does not mislead the jury. Prosecutors and defense attorneys sometimes try to simplify information for the jury, said Valerio, but this approach can result in a misstatement of the scientific conclusion.

Preparation and training of attorneys is thus critical to the accurate conveyance of the results of advanced forensic DNA technologies in the courtroom, Valerio explained. He noted that select jurisdictions require prosecutors to complete training in forensic evidence, pointing to the National District Attorneys Association as one source of this training for prosecutors. Valerio concluded by calling for attorneys to increase their understanding of PG and statistics, while recognizing that the scientist on the stand is the expert.

Clark agreed that attempts to simplify the findings of advanced forensic DNA technologies usually result in overcomplication. It is the expert scientist's responsibility to educate the judge or jury, she explained, and attorneys' attempts at simplification can necessitate further clarification from the scientist. Clark pointed out that this issue is compounded by a training gap within the forensic science community. Biologists and DNA analysts are not inherently statisticians, and they too may misstate results when attempting to simplify. Additionally, varying laws and practices across jurisdictions mean that evidence must be presented differently, requiring attorneys and scientific experts to be well informed and prepared for these requirements. Clark underscored the importance of pretrial collaboration among attorneys and experts to ensure shared understanding of forensic results, and as a space with room for improvement in the implementation of advanced forensic DNA technologies.

Audience Questions

During the Q&A section, Martschenko responded to a proposal for a "victim-centered" approach to implementing advanced forensic DNA technologies. She suggested that "victims" could also include those who are unnecessarily and adversely impacted by the criminal justice system; she asked stakeholders to consider that while the success stories of using advanced forensic DNA technologies to solve crimes are easy to find, it is harder to see the hidden victims who have been unjustly arrested or incarcerated. Clark responded that while wrongful involvement in the criminal legal system is a risk, these technologies can also be used to exonerate innocent individuals. She suggested that using these technologies more broadly outside of the crime investigation arena—such as to identify missing persons or to exonerate—could help illustrate the benefits of the technologies and indicated that more funding could be warranted to expand the scope of access of these tools to populations that have historically faced adversity within the criminal legal system.

During the question-and-answer session, Erin Murphy, New York University—a workshop panelist and audience participant—questioned the statement that PG results are more accurate and consistent than previous methods. She said that through her legal work as well as reviews of the literature, she has observed large variation across laboratories and across analytical threshold choices. She noted that there are many choices to make in using PG, including which software to use, whether an allele is drop-in or drop-out,[6] and which population frequency files to use, and suggested that these choices can result in very different output. Murphy noted that these choices could be made based on the desired result, for example, setting a threshold so that it doesn't exclude the suspect. She asked the panelists for their thoughts on this observed variation. Clark responded that analytical thresholds are very dependent on the physical environment and specific instrument that are used and set as a product of each laboratory's validation, which makes interlaboratory comparisons difficult. Some variables and choices are unlikely to make a big difference to the results—such as choice of population frequency database used—while other variables have not yet been addressed by the forensic community. For example, the qualitative interpretation of a result could vary between analysts; one might conclude that a result provides "strong evidence" in support of a hypothesis, while another concludes that it is "very strong evidence." The onus is on the forensic science community, said Clark, to conduct more training on how to explain results not as absolutes but on a continuum.

---

[6] An *allele* is a variant form of a gene at a specific locus on a chromosome. More specifically, it is one of two or more versions of a DNA sequence that can occur at a given genomic location. Individuals inherit two alleles for each gene, one from each parent. These alleles can be identical (homozygous) or different (heterozygous; National Human Genome Research Institute [NHGRI], 2024). Alleles contribute to the genetic diversity within a population and can influence various traits, including physical characteristics, disease susceptibility, and responses to environmental factors. The interaction between different alleles can result in dominant, recessive, or codominant expression of traits (NHGRI, 2024). Allele drop-in and drop-out are phenomena that can occur during DNA amplification and analysis, particularly in forensic genetics. *Allele drop-out* refers to the failure of an allele to amplify during a polymerase chain reaction, resulting in its absence from the final DNA profile, which can lead to false homozygous results or partial profiles (Shestak et al., 2021). *Allele drop-in*, on the other hand, is the appearance of an additional allele in a DNA profile that does not belong to the true contributor(s) of the sample, often caused by contamination, artifacts in the amplification process, or stochastic effects in low-template DNA analysis (Gill et al., 2012).

2

Forensic Investigative Genetic Genealogy

OVERVIEW OF FORENSIC INVESTIGATIVE GENETIC GENEALOGY (FIGG)

In this session, panelists shared presentations on FIGG and spoke to various aspects of its use by law enforcement, including its process, benefits, challenges, ethical considerations, and the need for standards and regulations (see Box 2-1). With moderation by Heather McKiernan, RTI International, the session featured panelists with expertise in forensic science, law, medical ethics, and health policy.

Ray Wickenheiser, New York State Police Crime Lab System, began the session by reiterating earlier commentary from the law enforcement perspectives panel, calling attention to how FIGG is meant to be used by law enforcement only once other investigative methods have been exhausted on major violent crimes like homicides and sexual assaults where the suspect is still at large. He explained that after developing a DNA profile from crime scene evidence and getting no hits in Combined DNA Index System (CODIS) databases, the DNA is sent out for single nucleotide polymorphism (SNP) analysis to search commercial genealogical databases for potential familial matches. Echoing previous law enforcement representatives, Wickenheiser suggested that surviving victims and family members be considered in deliberations around the use of advanced forensic DNA technologies. FIGG also may be used in cases of missing persons or unidentified human remains, said Wickenheiser. This can generate investigative leads by building family trees from distant relatives, he explained. Wickenheiser argued that FIGG is scientifically and technically sound, with limitations, and that its use by law

BOX 2-1
Overview of Forensic Investigative Genetic Genealogy

The following overview reflects information shared in presentations from multiple workshop speakers. They should not be construed as consensus or exhaustive definitions of the topics discussed

What is it? *Forensic investigative genetic genealogy* (FIGG)* is a multistep, multidisciplinary process that combines advanced DNA analysis, genetic genealogy databases, and traditional genealogical methods to generate investigative leads and putative identities for previously unknown DNA samples.

How does it work? FIGG utilizes advanced DNA sequencing of evidence associated with a crime scene or unidentified remains to develop genetic profiles. Once a profile is generated, a genetic genealogist uploads it to an approved public genealogy database, which contains DNA profiles uploaded voluntarily by members of the public. The DNA profile is then compared to the database profiles to algorithmically find users who share segments of DNA with the unknown sample. A statistical calculation predicts the relationship type of the user to the sample (e.g., second cousin). Genealogical research and family tree building is then conducted to trace the family lineages of these matches, with the goal of identifying the unknown person by finding where lineages intersect and share a common ancestor.

Who is involved in its use? FIGG relies on collaboration between forensic labs, commercial vendors, genealogists, and law enforcement.

What is the scale of use? FIGG is an emerging technology that has seen rapid increases in use in the United States since its high-profile use in 2018 to identify the Golden State Killer suspect.

What regulations and/or guidelines apply to its use? The Department of Justice issued an interim policy in 2019 providing guidelines for the federal use of FIGG. The National Technology Validation and Implementation Collaborative released guidelines in 2023 providing comprehensive recommendations for establishing FIGG programs. In 2021, Maryland enacted the first state law specifically regulating FIGG (see Box 2-4), while states such as Utah and Florida have passed laws related to FIGG, addressing concepts such as genetic privacy and public records disclosure. Finally, genetic genealogy databases like GEDmatch, FamilyTreeDNA, and DNASolves have specific policies governing law enforcement use of their services for FIGG. In April 2024, the Investigative Genetic Genealogy Accreditation Board (2024) published updated professional standards and a code of ethics for FIGG practitioners.

---

*The DNA technologies discussed at the workshop are not referred to with consistent terminology by forensic, law enforcement, and legal experts, with multiple variations on the names of the technologies discussed at this workshop. For consistency, the terms *forensic investigative genetic genealogy*, *probabilistic genotyping software*, and *forensic DNA phenotyping* are used across these workshop proceedings.

SOURCE: Generated by the rapporteur based on workshop presentations from March 13 and 14, 2024.

enforcement to solve crimes is ethical if done with appropriate guardrails and informed consent from database participants.

Process of FIGG

Claire Glynn, University of New Haven, described FIGG as a multidisciplinary process, because it utilizes multiple technologies from the areas of genetic genealogy, consumer DNA testing, genealogical research, and forensic science to analyze matches and build family trees. Glynn noted that millions of people have sent DNA samples to consumer DNA websites. However, Glynn clarified that for the purposes of FIGG, only a small percentage of these samples are available for analysis by law enforcement. She explained that in the wake of the use of FIGG in the Golden State Killer investigation in 2018, several commercial DNA testing companies changed their terms of service and privacy policies to explicitly prohibit the use of their databases for law enforcement. However, she noted that both FamilyTreeDNA and GEDmatch allow the use of their databases for FIGG; together they have DNA information for about 4 million people. Both sites allow consumers to opt in or out of allowing their data to be used for law enforcement, said Glynn, so the number is somewhat smaller when accounting for those who have opted out.

Wickenheiser and Glynn went into further detail on the multidisciplinary FIGG process. First, evidence from the crime scene is analyzed by an internal or external laboratory that conducts SNP testing, said Wickenheiser. There are a few options for SNP testing, Glynn said; one option can be conducted in house and specifically eliminates the discovery of any health-related genetic information. Wickenheiser noted that traditional sample analysis that is used to look for direct matches in the CODIS uses short tandem repeat (STR) analysis, while SNP analysis is used to look for kinship matches in a genealogical database.[1] The DNA file is uploaded to one of the genealogy websites using a law enforcement–specific portal, said Glynn, and an algorithm compares the data with user data and looks for matching SNPs. The results give information about the amount of shared DNA, and a statistical calculation determines the potential relationship type to the person of interest (e.g., second cousin). Results may also provide information about the potential ancestry of the person of interest, she

---

[1] SNPs and STRs are both genetic markers used in forensic DNA analysis, but they differ significantly in their structure, applications, and advantages. STRs are the primary markers used in forensic DNA profiling for human identification, paternity testing, and linking suspects to crime scenes. They are the basis for national DNA databases like CODIS (Butler, 2006; Federal Bureau of Investigation, n.d.-b; National Institute of Justice, 2011). SNPs are useful for analyzing highly degraded DNA samples, predicting phenotypic traits (e.g., eye or hair), and providing information on biogeographical ancestry (Weir & Zheng, 2015).

explained. When kinship matches are identified, investigators can use these relative names to search publicly available information and begin to build family trees to identify a person of interest.

Glynn emphasized the importance of documenting every step of the FIGG process and using best practices and standards for genealogical research. Documentation serves as evidence that "the result was achieved in an ethical and responsible manner within the boundaries of all the laws and policies that exist," she said. The result of a FIGG analysis, Glynn continued, is the identification of a potential suspect and the use of traditional STR testing to exclude or include the person. If the STR profile from the crime scene does not match the person of interest, the investigator continues building the family tree and looking for other possibilities.

Before using FIGG, said Glynn, an investigator must ensure that the case type meets the criteria set by the U.S. Department of Justice (DOJ) guidelines and relevant state law (see Box 1-4 in Chapter 1). In addition, the case must meet the criteria for the use of the two genealogy databases. For the latter, the investigator must have already conducted traditional forensic DNA analysis consisting of STR testing and looking for matches in CODIS. If state law allows familial searching using STR profiles in the state DNA database, this search must also have been conducted. If there are no hits in CODIS, and no other investigative leads, FIGG may be conducted, said Glynn. She called for investigators to follow established genealogical standards, create quality assurance protocols specific to FIGG, increase education and awareness to encourage more people to opt in to databases, and balance protecting public safety with individual privacy through responsible and ethical use. Glynn offered the National Technology Validation and Implementation Collaborative guidelines for establishing FIGG programs as a source of valuable information on responsible and ethical implementation of FIGG programs (Wickenheiser et al., 2023). She also encouraged increased uploading of people's DNA into FIGG databases, so long as they have an informed understanding of what this process entails, considering the huge potential for FIGG to help prevent and solve crimes.

Distinct Characteristics of FIGG

Wickenheiser said that while FIGG involves many steps and interactions between multiple proven, traditional forensic and scientific technologies, it is essentially a new process of obtaining an investigative lead, which can eventually be confirmed through follow-up investigation and standard STR direct comparison. Erin Murphy, New York University School of Law, disagreed with this statement, suggesting that FIGG is "totally different" from traditional investigative methods and that these differences create real risks. Murphy described some of the major differences between FIGG and traditional forensic DNA analysis (Table 2-1). She explained that the DNA analyzed is different—traditional analysis looks at noncoding "junk" DNA, while FIGG uses SNP analysis that reveals many information-rich genes. Traditional forensic analysis is done in regulated government laboratories, whereas FIGG relies on largely unregulated technologies, she said. Traditional analysis implicates only the target suspect and a few closely related individuals, whereas FIGG brings potentially thousands of people into the investigation.

An individual's DNA contains information that is relevant not just to the moment that it is collected; it can also reveal information about prior generations and unborn descendants, said Murphy. She noted that this makes DNA different from other types of crime scene evidence, which do not provide investigators with such information. Furthermore, she said, as technology advances, a DNA sample gains more capacity to reveal sensitive information. If misuse by bad actors occurs, a person cannot revoke access to their or their ancestors' DNA. Finally, Murphy echoed Tsosie's comments from the opening session in noting that, unlike other types of crime scene evidence, DNA is monetizable and has tremendous value beyond crime-

TABLE 2-1 Differences Between Traditional Forensic DNA Analysis and Genetic Genealogy

	Traditional forensic DNA/CODIS system	Genetic Genealogy
Test type	• Non-coding, "junk" STR, ~20 loci (~10,000 bp of repeats)	• SNP, "gold," panels developed for biomedical research, ~600k to 1 million nucleotides (GTCA)
Analysis done by	• Government analysts in regulated government labs, or outsourced labs compliant with QAS	• Largely unregulated private, for-profit companies; private persons
Sample restrictions	• *Source*: putative perpetrator crime scene sample (no victims, clear non-suspects, non crime-scene evidence) • *Quality*: 8+ loci + rarity; single source or deconvolved or mixture under 4 alleles/loci • *Kits*: validated & standardized "profile" • *Kits*: validated within laboratory • *Lab/analyst*: CODIS QA/QC, including accreditation	• Site, vendor dependent; possibly none
Data storage	• Paperwork/documentation required • Audits for accuracy • No national storage of elimination samples, witnesses, or non-perpetrators • Decentralized data; pointer system	• Site, vendor, genealogist dependent; possibly none
Search restrictions	• Access limited to pre-qualified personnel • Criminal penalties for misuse	• Site, vendor, genealogist dependent and self-enforced by genealogists; possibly none
Privacy of target AND non-target others	• Weak ancestral, 1st degree relatives	• Biomedical information; possibly behavioral info • Detailed ancestral; links to thousands well beyond social family • Implicates ancestors and descendants

NOTE: bp = base pairs; CODIS = Combined DNA Index System; GTCA = guanine, thymine, cytosine, and adenine; QA/QC = quality assurance and control; QAS = quality assurance standards; STR = short tandem repeat.
SOURCE: Presented by Erin Murphy on March 13, 2024.

solving. To this point, Murphy noted that outside of law enforcement, a robust conversation is occurring about the risks of commercial DNA analysis; for example, the military has advised members not to use recreational DNA testing because of potential privacy and security risks.

Public Perspectives on FIGG

There is strong public support for FIGG, said Christi Guerrini, Baylor College of Medicine. Guerrini told workshop participants about her research on public and expert perceptions of FIGG and the policy implications of these perceptions. She presented empirical research from a national, representative sample showing strong and consistent public support for using FIGG to identify violent perpetrators, but less support for nonviolent crimes. She then explained that FIGG fundamentally relies on consumer DNA databases and these databases exist only if people contribute genetic samples and consent to their use by law enforcement. If database participants begin to have doubts about the use of FIGG, they might withdraw their consent or remove their DNA profiles. Experts are very aware of the need for public support, said Guerrini, and they support the creation of guardrails to ensure public trust in the technology.

Guerrini's study found that over 90% of the public support the use of FIGG to identify violent perpetrators, unidentified human remains, and unidentified babies, or to exonerate wrongfully convicted individuals (Figure 2-1). However, the level of support for FIGG drops to about 50% for its use to solve nonviolent crimes. There is broad public consensus around the need for regulation and oversight of FIGG, Guerrini reiterated.

Guerrini's research project also included input from a "policy Delphi," with 34 expert participants with backgrounds in law enforcement, forensic science, genealogy, law, ethics, and victim advocacy. In the policy Delphi, the experts came together several times over the course of a year to discuss, debate, and identify priority issues. The group identified nine priority issues in four areas (Figure 2-2), and then explored policy options in these areas. Guerrini provided details on two of the priority issues and the associated policy options. The Delphi experts agreed that patchwork governance is a major concern and identified four policy options: (a) a federal FIGG law, (b) state model laws, (c) a finalized DOJ policy, and (d) conditioning grants on best practice compliance. The second area of concern was law enforcement participating in databases against their terms of service. To address this issue, policy options included an outright ban on the practice, a standard database consent approach (e.g., all opt-in or all opt-out), and the development of a database that is used only by law enforcement that is populated with genetic profiles donated specifically for this purpose. Guerrini emphasized that the policy Delphi process included relevant parties from a broad

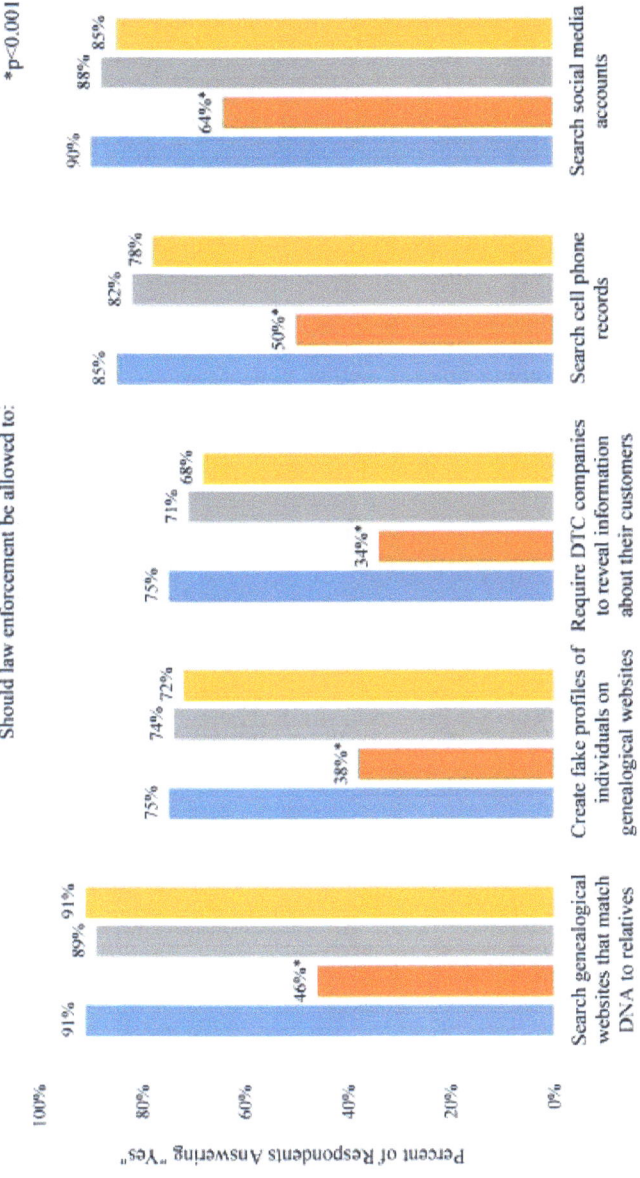

FIGURE 2-1 U.S. general population survey of support for forensic investigative genetic genealogy: 2018.
NOTE: DTC = direct-to-consumer.
SOURCE: Guerrini et al., under the terms of the Creative Commons Attribution License (CC BY). (2018): https://doi.org/10.1371/journal.pbio.2006906

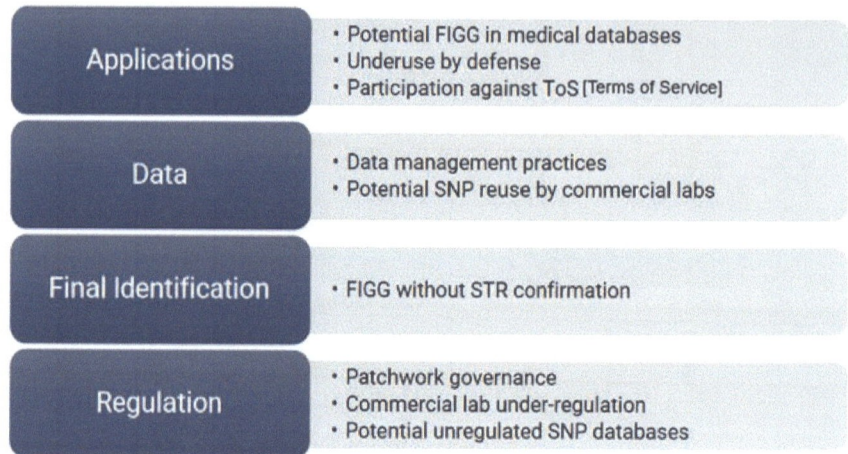

FIGURE 2-2 Nine priority issues for FIGG as identified by policy Delphi.
NOTE: FIGG = forensic investigative genetic genealogy; SNP = single nucleotide polymorphism; STR = short tandem repeat.
SOURCE: Presentation by Christi Guerrini, March 13, 2024.

spectrum of fields. She echoed discussions from the previous two panels when reiterating that any policymaking in this area should similarly be informed by a diverse group.

CONSIDERATIONS FOR USE OF FIGG BY LAW ENFORCEMENT

Opportunities

Wickenhauser and Glynn mirrored the previous panel in emphasizing the significant benefits of FIGG in solving cold cases and enhancing public safety (see Box 2-2). Wickenhauser noted that FIGG has been instrumental in identifying perpetrators who might otherwise remain at large, thereby preventing future crimes. Glynn highlighted the success of FIGG in identifying a perpetrator in more than 1,000 cases, demonstrating its potential to resolve many more with increased public participation and funding. Before speakers addressed the ethical challenges and scientific limitations of FIGG, Wickenheiser clarified what he considered to be ethically sound components of FIGG. He argued that individuals have no right to privacy regarding forensic evidence discarded at a crime scene and reminded the audience that these forms of forensic evidence have been collected and analyzed to solve crimes for decades. In addition, he noted that databases and public records

BOX 2-2
Opportunities and Challenges in Using FIGG Identified by Workshop Speakers

Opportunities

Solving cold cases: FIGG has been instrumental in identifying perpetrators who might otherwise remain at large. (Wickenhauser, Clark, Valerio, Pooley, Katz, & Belli)

Enhancing public safety: Identifying perpetrators who would otherwise be at large has the potential to prevent future crimes. (Wickenhauser & Glynn)

Established and reliable methods: Both short tandem repeat and single nucleotide polymorphism analysis used in FIGG are well-established, reliable methods of analyzing DNA, ensuring scientific soundness in kinship matching. (Wickenhauser, Tripplet, Clark, & Belli)

Challenges

Limitations of consent: The traditional model of individual consent does not address the unique nature of DNA, as individuals upload their DNA without consideration of implications of relatives, who have not consented to be part of a database. (Murphy, Tsosie, Martschenko, & Lynch)

Disparate impact: FIGG can be costly and may be implemented inequitably, resulting in unequal access to advanced crime-solving tools in under-resourced areas. (Wickenhauser, Bradford, Pooley, & Tsosie)

Privacy and intrusiveness: FIGG investigations can become overbroad and intrusive, with genealogists sometimes breaking rules without consequences, leading to ethical concerns. (Murphy, Tsosie, & Martschenko)

Undermining public trust: The use of forensic DNA technologies for law enforcement purposes can undermine public trust in DNA analysis for health risks, particularly in communities with historic mistrust of the health care system and law enforcement. (Murphy, Bradford, Clark, Pooley, & Tsosie)

Spillover effects on public safety: Fear of genetic information misuse could discourage crime victims from reporting incidents or participating in DNA analysis, thereby impacting public safety. (Murphy, Tsosie, Lynch, Clark, & Martschenko)

SOURCE: Generated by the rapporteur based on workshop presentations from March 13 and 14, 2024.

are routinely used to solve crimes. What is new with FIGG, he said, is the use of databases with information on relatives. With informed consent, however, Wickenheiser said that public databases can be used ethically in FIGG. He added that people have the right to make any use of their own DNA, including helping law enforcement solve crimes.

Challenges and Ethical Considerations

Reliability and Limitations

One major risk of any new technology, said Wickenheiser, is whether it is reliable and accurate. The process of FIGG encompasses several technologies and approaches, so its reliability is dependent on the reliability of these underlying approaches. There may be limitations to the utility of FIGG if the sample at the crime scene has issues with quantity, quality, or mixtures of samples. If crime scene DNA is of limited quantity or quality, said Glynn, it may not be appropriate to utilize all of it for FIGG. Wickenheiser said that both STR and SNP analysis are well-established and reliable methods of analyzing DNA. He explained that kinship matching via DNA is a scientifically sound practice, although genealogical and public databases that are used to find relatives may have errors or omissions. Wickenheiser emphasized that any leads gathered through this process must ultimately be confirmed with STR direct comparison, which he said is an established, accurate, and reliable method of forensic evidence analysis.

Murphy disagreed with Wickenheiser's assertion that FIGG and its underlying testing are always reliable, raising concerns about the legitimate risks of FIGG use. She said that DNA testing always involves the risk of wrongful arrest and detention, and she illustrated this reality by outlining a case in Washington where Joao Monterio was wrongly arrested for a 25-year-old cold case based on a genealogical profile built using DNA from the crime scene (Carter, 2024; *Monterio v. Cormier*). He was released after spending three-and-a-half years in jail, during which time he lost his job and his wife died (Carter, 2024). In another case, Murphy highlighted, a man was charged with murder because his DNA was found on the fingernails of the decedent (Worth, 2018). Because it was a death penalty–eligible case, his attorney accessed his medical records to look for mitigation factors. He found that the man had been in a detox center at the time of the murder and the DNA had likely been transferred via a pulse oximeter (Worth, 2018). Murphy said that these cases demonstrate that advanced forensic DNA technologies, even with "reliable" STR confirmation, can result in innocent people being arrested. There are other anecdotes like these, said Murphy, but it is difficult to know the true extent of mistakes because of a lack of systematic information about the use of advanced forensic DNA technologies.

Informed Consent

Murphy pushed back against Wickenheiser's conceptualization of informed consent, suggesting that using an informed consent model analogous to that used for research is misguided in the case of FIGG. She noted that when one uploads their DNA to a website, they are consenting to the matching of their own DNA—not their brother's, children's, or cousin's. However, she advised that the nature of DNA data creates opportunities for FIGG investigations to become overbroad and intrusive, when considering factors such as their ability to trace distant relatives, the realities of routine rule-breaking by genealogists with little consequence, and the surreptitious DNA sampling of third parties. The consent model is a fiction, she said, because FIGG is used specifically to find people who are not in the database and who did not consent.

Disparate Impact

Another risk of FIGG and other forensic DNA technologies, said Wickenheiser, is the potential for it to be used in an inequitable way or to have a disparate impact. Greater than 80% of crimes are conducted by individuals within the same socioeconomic group as the victim, he said. When choosing to use limited resources on tools like FIGG, it is important that cases are chosen in an equitable fashion, and resources are deployed to solve crimes in disadvantaged areas. Furthermore, Wickenheiser said, there is an ethical imperative to use FIGG and other technologies to find perpetrators who are still at large, as well as to exonerate wrongfully suspected or incarcerated individuals. Advanced forensic DNA technologies should be applied to all unsolved cases equitably and quickly, he said, because unsolved cases are a major public safety issue.

Scope of Use and Impact

The use of FIGG brings up concerns about overbroad and intrusive investigations, said Murphy, with a lack of accountability and incentives to break rules and push ethical boundaries. The limited rules that have been put into place have been broken with little consequence, she said, and law enforcement officials have engaged in behavior that many would consider unethical, including

- going beyond terms of service to get access to data;
- using a fake name and account to access data;
- surreptitiously sampling many nonsuspects and suspects in order to speed up the investigation; and
- retaining elaborate family trees in law enforcement databases.

Murphy added that using forensic DNA technologies like FIGG presents the risk of spillover effects, such as undermining public health benefits of DNA analysis. People may be hesitant to have their DNA analyzed for health risks if they fear that their information will be used for law enforcement purposes; this risk is particularly relevant in communities of color where there is historic mistrust of both the health care system and law enforcement. There are also risks to public safety, said Murphy. For example, a rape victim may refuse to report her rape and do a rape kit for fears that her genetic information will be used to implicate herself or a relative.

Considerations for Implementation

Like all powerful technologies, said Wickenheiser, FIGG should be implemented using established best practices. He suggested that FIGG best practices would include accreditation to ensure quality of testing, a system of oversight, terms of service for databases with penalties for misuse, and the proper handling of DNA samples from all parties. Wickenheiser pointed to the published National Technology Validation and Implementation Collaborative (NTVIC) guidelines that describe appropriate guidelines, policies, and procedures for the use of FIGG (Box 2-3; Wickenheiser et al., 2023). In order to follow these best practices, he said, training and education will be necessary for investigators and other parties within the legal system.

Many people have described FIGG as the "Wild West" of emerging forensic DNA technologies, said Glynn, but she said that there are now "some reins on the horse." For the first few years, forensic scientists were "building the plane while they were flying it" because there were no rule book or protocols to follow. Now, she said, there is a road map of how a FIGG case should be carried out, who should be involved, and the NTVIC guidelines to follow (Wickenheiser et al., 2023). Since forensic DNA was first used in 1984, training, education, and method validation have been critical to ensuring its reliability and appropriate use, said Glynn. With FIGG, the same process should be applied. Adhering to policies, laws, and standards is essential for fulfilling the potential of the technology, as well as for maintaining public trust and protecting the privacy and safety of the public.

Several speakers in this and the previous session referred to Maryland Criminal Procedure § 17-102 (2024; see Box 2-4), with both Murphy and

> **BOX 2-3**
> **Guidelines for Establishing FIGG Programs**
>
> NTVIC established guidance on appropriate guidelines, policies, and procedures for the use of FIGG.
>
> **Purpose:** The document provides guidelines and considerations for public and private crime laboratories and investigative agencies to establish FIGG programs.
>
> **Scope:** FIGG utilizes single nucleotide polymorphism DNA profiles generated by next-generation sequencing and established genetic and genealogical research methodologies to generate investigative leads in unsolved investigations, such as missing persons and violent crimes.
>
> **Goals:** The guidelines aim to share minimum standards and best practices for optimizing resources, promoting technology implementation, and evaluating the quality of forensic investigations.
>
> **Critical parties:** The guidelines were developed with input from various parties, including federal, state, and local government crime laboratory leaders, university researchers, and private technology and research companies.
>
> **Legislation and policy:** The NTVIC guidelines incorporate feedback from stakeholders and are updated as needed based on new legislation introduced or passed since the original publication.
>
> **Implementation:** Each jurisdiction is responsible for its own program policy, but the guidelines promote sharing practices and processes to enable the implementation of new forensic technology.
>
> **Collaborative efforts:** The NTVIC was established to collaborate nationally on validation, method development, and implementation in forensic science.
>
> **Additional resources:** The guidelines reference other important documents and policies, such as the U.S. Department of Justice's (2019) Interim Policy on Forensic Genetic Genealogical DNA Analysis and Searching.
>
> SOURCE: Wickenheiser et al., 2023.

BOX 2-4
Maryland Code, Criminal Procedure § 17-102

Maryland Code, Criminal Procedure § 17-102 (2024), establishes state-level regulations for investigations using FIGG. These regulations ensure that FIGG investigations are conducted with judicial oversight, respect for privacy, and strict adherence to legal and ethical standards. The following lists key provisions:

Requirement for judicial authorization: FIGG investigations cannot be initiated without judicial authorization. A prosecutor must certify before the court that the investigation meets specific criteria, including the nature of the crime and the exhaustion of other investigative methods.

Sworn affidavit: A law enforcement agent, with the approval of a prosecutor, must submit a sworn affidavit to the court demonstrating that (a) the crime involves murder, rape, a felony sexual offense, or a criminal act posing a substantial and ongoing threat to public safety or national security; (b) the forensic sample is biological material reasonably believed to be connected to the crime scene, a person, an item, or a location related to the criminal event, or the unidentified remains of a suspected homicide victim; (c) an single tandem repeat DNA profile has been developed from the forensic sample, entered into state and national DNA databases, and failed to identify a known individual; and (d) reasonable investigative leads have been pursued and failed to identify the perpetrator, unless the crime presents an ongoing threat to public safety or national security.

Licensed laboratory: The laboratory conducting single nucleotide polymorphism/sequencing testing for FIGG must be licensed by the state.

Licensing program: The Maryland Department of Health's Office of Health Care Quality is responsible for establishing licensing requirements for laboratories and individuals performing genetic genealogy. This includes developing best practices and training programs.

Restrictions on use of biological samples: Biological samples subjected to FIGG DNA analysis cannot be used to determine the sample donor's genetic predisposition for disease or any other medical condition.

Database requirements: FIGG investigations can use only direct-to-consumer or publicly available open-data personal genomics databases that (a) provide explicit notice to users that law enforcement may use their services; and (b) seek acknowledgment and express consent from users regarding this notice.

Informed consent from third parties: Written consent is required for collecting DNA samples from third parties (nonsuspects), documented by video or audio. If a third party refuses, law enforcement may seek a court order for covert collection, provided it is necessary and minimizes intrusiveness.

Data handling: Upon completion of a FIGG investigation without prosecution, acquittal, or after sentencing/appeals, the court must order (a) destruction of all DNA samples and genetic genealogy data derived from the FIGG analysis, (b) removal of any uploaded FIGG profiles from databases, and (c) destruction of data from individuals not identified as the source of the crime scene DNA. Genealogists cannot retain any records/materials from the FIGG investigation.

Prohibited disclosures: Unauthorized disclosure of genetic genealogy data, FIGG profiles, or DNA samples is prohibited. Violators are guilty of a misdemeanor and subject to imprisonment and fines.

Failure to destroy data: Willful failure to destroy genetic genealogy information, FIGG profiles, or DNA samples as required is also a misdemeanor, with similar penalties.

Private right of action: Individuals whose genetic genealogy information is wrongfully disclosed, collected, or maintained have a private right of action and are entitled to minimum liquidated damages of $5,000 per violation.

Defense access for exonerative purposes: Defendants charged or convicted of a violent crime can request permission from a judge to use FIGG testing to help prove their innocence, both pre- and post-trial.

Annual reporting requirements: The Governor's Office of Crime Prevention, Youth, and Victim Services must prepare and submit an annual report regarding requests for forensic genetic genealogical analysis, reviewed by a panel of stakeholders who make policy recommendations. These reports are publicly accessible and can be found on the Governor's Office of Crime Prevention, Youth, and Victim Services webpage for 2021, 2022, and 2023 (Maryland Governor's Office of Crime Prevention and Policy, n.d.).

SOURCE: Maryland Criminal Procedure Code, 2024.

Dan Katz, Maryland State Police Forensic Sciences Division, commending the collaborative process that led to its development and adoption. Murphy said that while she would have preferred an outright ban on FIGG, she views both the process and the outcome as good. The law is a comprehensive regime, and it includes the voices and perspectives of many stakeholders. In response to a question, Murphy described some of the components of the law. A warrant is required to begin the process of FIGG, which means there is judicial oversight from the beginning. Under the law, FIGG is treated as a "last resort as opposed to first option," said Murphy. It requires following the rules of databases, and explicit notice and informed consent of nonsuspects or nontargets. There are public reporting and data requirements, and a route allowing for the defense to get access to the technology. Murphy said that law enforcement needs to provide information about return on investment when the public is paying for advanced forensic DNA technologies; tracking metrics about the use of these technologies is critical for understanding how and when they are used, and these are "not super complicated questions." The Maryland law also requires that laboratories and genealogists be licensed, said Murphy, but the licensing system does not yet exist. Some stakeholders have complained that this is going to "put the brakes" on FIGG because it will take a long time to ramp up; Murphy said that taking time to do things properly is how it should be when implementing new technologies.

Currently, many rules around FIGG are simply "the fox guarding the hen house," said Murphy. Instead of these self-regulations, she called for laws to be developed through a democratic process with the involvement of relevant parties; she indicated that these laws should have accountability mechanisms to incentivize proper utilization and disincentivize misuse.

In response to a question from a workshop audience member, panelists identified several essential components of appropriate and ethical implementation of FIGG, many of which are directly reflected in Maryland Code, Criminal Procedure § 17-102 (2024) and Utah Public Safety Code 53-10-403.7 (2023):

- a diverse set of stakeholders to set policies (Wickenheiser & Glynn);
- a unified system of overarching guidelines, with room for state differences (Wickenheiser);
- laboratory accreditation (Wickenheiser);
- support from the federal government to bring together stakeholders (Glynn & Guerrini);
- data transparency (Murphy);
- acknowledgment of the power systems at play (Tsosie); and
- education and engagement with the public (Guerrini).

REFLECTIONS

Following the four panelist presentations, Krystal Tsosie, Arizona State University and the discussant for this session, offered her reflections on the discussion around FIGG. The use of FIGG, she said, is not devoid of complex cultural, ethical, societal, and legal concerns. Recalling a statement by Wickenheiser about the high percentage of crimes in which the victim and the perpetrator are from the same economic class, Tsosie said that it is easier for tribal people to justify the use of forensics when violence is perpetrated onto Indigenous women by nontribal members. However, when violence is perpetrated by members of one's own community, it creates "uncomfortable questions" about the use of the community's genetic information to solve crimes. Another issue that stood out for Tsosie was the discussion around storing DNA indefinitely to use it in the future with more advanced technologies. She noted that every time the technology improves, the risks to privacy for individuals and communities increase. "We need to answer questions about how long it is appropriate to store DNA, who has access to it, and what standards are used for future testing. For genetic information that is held by commercial DNA testing companies, what safety measures are put in place to ensure that the DNA is used for the purposes for which consent was given? What happens when companies are bought and sold? Do the privacy protections and terms of service follow the data?"

A variety of people is involved in the process of FIGG, said Tsosie, and it is not clear what training they have, whether they are certified, and if their expertise is validated. Who are considered "FIGG experts," she asked, and what communities do they or do they not represent? Are there FIGG ethical and professional standards, and if so, who is writing these standards? Murphy noted during her talk that there are multiple instances of people involved in FIGG breaking their own rules with no consequence.

Finally, Tsosie addressed the fact that genetic databases do not reflect the general population. Incarcerated individuals are disproportionately likely to come from communities of color (National Academies of Sciences, Engineering, and Medicine, 2023). As a result, they are also overrepresented in criminal DNA databases, so the use of such databases can exacerbate racial injustices. Genealogy databases have less information on historically marginalized populations, in particular Native Americans. This is the result of complex sociopolitical processes, and it is not going to be solved by simply encouraging people to provide their DNA to the system, she said. Tsosie asked how to ensure that advanced forensic DNA technologies ameliorate rather than exacerbate inequities, and how to ensure that they are used with respect for individual and community autonomy. She noted that there are no easy answers to these questions, but that the discussions at the workshop generate necessary conversations around these issues.

3

Probabilistic Genotyping

This workshop session focused on probabilistic genotyping (PG; see Box 3-1) and featured presentations from panelists with expertise in forensic analysis, genetics, computer science, and law. It was moderated by Alicia Carriquiry, Iowa State University. Panelists called attention to various aspects of the use of PG in law enforcement, including its processes, benefits, challenges, and the need for standards and regulations.

OVERVIEW OF PG

Craig O'Connor, New York City Office of the Chief Medical Examiner, provided a brief overview of PG for workshop attendees and participants. He explained that PG helps police, laboratory, and forensic professionals compare DNA found at crime scenes with that of potential suspects, even when the DNA is limited in quality, damaged, or mixed from different people. Todd Bille, National Laboratory Center of the U.S. Bureau of Alcohol, Tobacco, Firearms and Explosives, explained that PG is utilized broadly to obtain the most information possible from a DNA profile. He stated that PG involves the multidisciplinary use of biological modeling, statistical theory, computer algorithms, and probability distributions to analyze forensic DNA samples. PG combines these tools to calculate likeli-

BOX 3-1
Overview of Probabilistic Genotyping and Related Software

The following overview reflects information shared in presentations from multiple workshop speakers. They should not be construed as consensus or exhaustive definitions of the topics discussed.

What is it? *Probabilistic genotyping* (PG) is a forensic tool conducted using probabilistic genotyping software to analyze and interpret complex DNA evidence from crime scenes (e.g., DNA samples that include multiple sources, are limited in quantity, and/or are damaged). It employs advanced statistical modeling and computer algorithms to assess the strength of evidence given two potential scenarios, such as whether DNA from the person of interest is present in the sample, or not. PG has two main functions: (a) mixture deconvolution to determine what genotypes could be contributors to a sample and (b) calculation of the statistical weight of a comparison to a person of interest.

How does it work? Forensic investigators collect DNA from crime scene evidence and from a person of interest as a reference sample. Investigators then generate DNA profiles, which show peaks that represent the varying lengths of DNA fragments. PG runs computer simulations of many different scenarios, comparing the evidence DNA profile with the person of interest's profile and that of other potential contributors, and calculates two probabilities: (a) the likelihood that the evidence DNA would match if the person of interest contributed to the sample, and (b) the likelihood that the evidence DNA would match if the person of interest did not contribute. By comparing these probabilities, investigators can assess the strength of evidence linking or excluding the person of interest to the crime scene sample.

Who is involved in its use? The software used in PG is typically developed and sold by commercial vendors to forensic laboratories/analysts and internally validated by individual labs.

What is the scale of use? PG has been generally accepted, widely adopted, and used by over 100 law enforcement and/or state labs in the United States.

What regulations and/or guidelines apply to its use? The Federal Bureau of Investigation's Quality Assurance Standards, which became effective as of July 2020, provide guidelines for forensic DNA testing laboratories. While not specifically mentioning PG, they cover validation requirements for new methodologies used in DNA analysis. The Scientific Working Group on DNA Analysis Methods (2023) guidelines (see Box 3-2) provide detailed recommendations for labs implementing PG. ANSI/ADB Standard 018, published in 2020, sets forth specific requirements for the validation of probabilistic genotyping systems.

---

*The DNA technologies discussed at the workshop are not referred to with consistent terminology by forensic, law enforcement, and legal experts, with multiple variations on the names of the technologies discussed at this workshop. For consistency, the terms *forensic investigative genetic genealogy*, *probabilistic genotyping software*, and *forensic DNA phenotyping* are used across these workshop proceedings.

SOURCE: Definitions presented by Heather McKiernan and Craig O'Connor on March 13, 2024.

hood ratios[1] and/or infer genotypes for the DNA typing results of forensic samples. Bille pointed to the Scientific Working Group on DNA Analysis Methods (SWGDAM, 2023) *Guidelines for the Validation of Probabilistic Genotyping Systems*, which include a formal definition of PG and a framework for forensic laboratories to validate PG (see Box 3-2). PG has two main functions, he explained:

1. mixture deconvolution, which results in a list of possible contributing genotypes and their associated weights or probabilities, and
2. calculating the statistical weight of a sample compared with the DNA of a person of interest, based on relevant population databases.

The results of PG could indicate a very high likelihood ratio for a person who is included in a forensic sample, Bille said. He explained that PG also has the ability to discriminate between true contributors and non-contributors to a mixed DNA profile. PG makes more efficient use of the data present in the DNA profile and can potentially provide evidence of exclusion for individuals who may not have been excluded with previous technologies. PG is less subjective than other technologies, which, argued Bille, allows for greater consistency over time within the laboratory and between analysts within the lab.

The forensic community is quickly adopting PG, with the number of laboratories using PG increasing from around 10 in 2016 to almost 90 in 2023 (Figure 3-1). Bille noted that training is essential for the proper use of PG because the software is not automatically configured for use and requires individuals with knowledge and skill to properly implement and maintain. Analysts need to be trained in DNA interpretation and manual deconvolution of mixtures so that they can compare the outputs of PG with what would logically be expected based on validated parameters. If the output from the software does not match what the analyst would expect, the analyst should be able to detect the problem and identify what went wrong, said Bille. If the software models the DNA profile incorrectly (e.g., produces a list of possible genotypes and associated weights that do not properly reflect the DNA profile content) and this goes unnoticed by the analyst, inaccurate conclusions may be reported.

---

[1] *Likelihood ratios* are statistical assessments of the strength of evidence given two potential scenarios or propositions. For example, in a criminal case involving a person of interest, a forensic laboratory may assess the strength of evidence that a person of interest did contribute to a DNA sample found at a crime scene, compared with the strength of evidence that they did not contribute to that sample. PG thus does not result in a binary yes/no inclusion or exclusion of an individual from a forensic DNA sample; instead, it results in a likelihood ratio that must be interpreted by the forensic analyst.

BOX 3-2
SWGDAM Guidelines for Validating Probabilistic Genotyping Systems

The SWGDAM *Guidelines for the Validation of Probabilistic Genotyping Systems* (2023) refer to *PG* as software and/or hardware that uses biological modeling, statistical theory, algorithms, and probability distributions to infer genotypes from DNA data and calculate likelihood ratios for that data under different propositions or hypotheses. The SWGDAM guidelines also contain a framework for forensic laboratories to validate PG software. These guidelines, summarized here, help ensure that the software is reliable, accurate, and suitable for forensic casework.

- Laboratories must validate PG systems prior to use for casework through both developmental and internal validation studies.
- Developmental validation studies should demonstrate that the software is performing calculations correctly for simple scenarios like single-source samples and two-person mixtures.
- Internal validation studies should assess the software's performance on more complex/challenging samples representative of typical casework, including:
  - varying template amounts (high and low)
  - varying mixture ratios
  - varying number of contributors
  - degraded/inhibited samples
  - sensitivity and specificity for detecting true contributors versus noncontributors
- Validation should determine the limitations and boundaries where the software produces reliable results.
- Validation data should inform the lab's standard operating procedures and interpretation protocols.
- Validation studies should compare performance with previous interpretation methods used by the lab.
- Validation should assess precision by examining reproducibility of results on the same samples.
- Guidelines provide a framework, but labs must determine appropriate sample numbers/types for their internal validation based on their intended use.

SOURCE: SWGDAM, 2023.

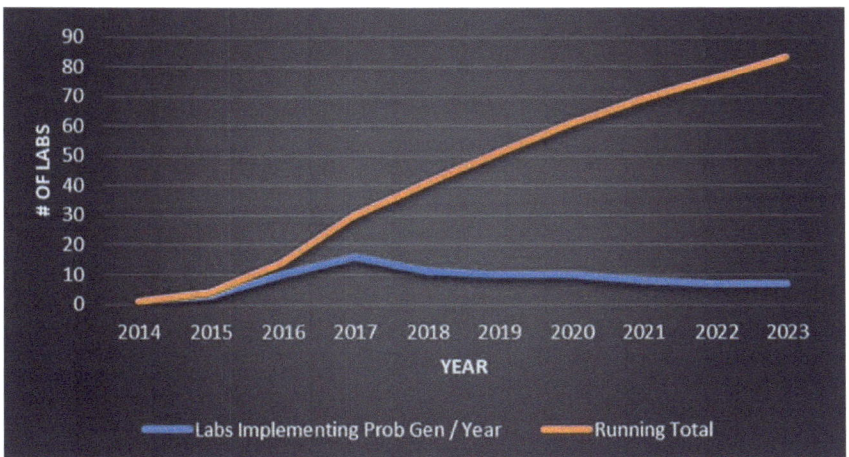

FIGURE 3-1 Implementation of probabilistic genotyping, 2014–2023.
SOURCE: Presented by Todd Bille on March 13, 2024.

Speakers explained that PG software creates detailed mathematical models that capture the characteristics of the DNA data obtained from the laboratory, such as peak heights, stutter patterns, and other artifacts. This modeling process is specific to each lab's procedures and instrumentation. The software quickly and simultaneously considers various factors, such as potential contributors, DNA template amounts, degradation, inhibition, and stochastic effects. After modeling the DNA data and accounting for the various factors, the software calculates likelihood ratios that provide a statistical assessment of the weight of the DNA evidence under different propositions (e.g., whether a person of interest contributed to the DNA mixture).

CONSIDERATIONS FOR PG USE BY LAW ENFORCEMENT

Opportunities

Considering what makes PG different from other advanced forensic DNA analysis tools, Bille noted that using PG can enable greater differentiation between DNA profiles (see Box 3-3). This can allow for the exclusion of people from a forensic sample who may not have been excluded with previous, less precise, technologies. Bille also noted that PG is less subjective than other forensic DNA analysis tools, which allows for the potential of greater consistency over time from individual analysts and across laboratories generally.

> **BOX 3-3**
> **Opportunities and Challenges in Using PG Identified by Workshop Speakers**
>
> **Opportunities**
>
> **Greater differentiation and precision:** PG can enable more precise differentiation between DNA profiles, allowing for the exclusion of individuals from forensic samples who may not have been excluded with previous, less precise technologies. (Clark, Triplett, & Bille)
>
> **Consistency and objectivity:** PG is less subjective than other forensic DNA analysis tools, which allows for greater consistency over time from individual analysts and across laboratories generally. (Bille & Pooley)
>
> **Crime solving:** PG can be particularly helpful in solving crimes, especially violent crimes, by providing more information for juries to evaluate the totality of evidence in a case, helping to determine guilt beyond a reasonable doubt. (Valerio, Pooley, & Clark)
>
> **Challenges**
>
> **Complexity and training:** PG requires more understanding, education, and training than other methods for estimating the statistical weight of evidence for forensic DNA profiles. This complexity is a challenge for laypersons, attorneys, and analysts. (Rudin, Belli, Clark, & Valerio)
>
> **Legal preparation:** Proper training and preparation for attorneys to accurately present statistical evidence in court are essential for the effective implementation of PG. (Wexler & Valerio)

Rebecca Wexler, University of California, Berkeley, stated that PG could be helpful in solving crimes. She pointed out that PG can provide more information for juries to evaluate the totality of evidence in a case. Wexler also stressed the need for proper training and preparation for attorneys to accurately present statistical evidence in court and noted that the implementation of PG is not without its challenges and ethical considerations.

Challenges and Ethical Considerations

Understanding and Education

Discussing the risks around use of PG, Norah Rudin, Forensic DNA Consulting, explained that PG requires more understanding, education, and training than other methods for estimating the statistical weight of evidence

Public understanding: A lack of public understanding of PG is a key challenge, necessitating better education and training for both the forensic science and legal communities to ensure accurate communication of PG results. (Rudin, Valerio, Martschenko, Pooley, O'Connor, & Clark)

Standardization, oversight, and accountability: Variations can occur due to random sampling during the DNA amplification process, which can lead to different results from the same sample. Human factors, such as choosing the analytical threshold, can also significantly impact results. Analytical thresholds are generally implemented via policies without standardization or adequate accountability mechanisms, affecting the final PG results. Reducing variation and setting a standard of practice require oversight and accountability systems. (Rudin, Katz, & Chu)

Verification and validation: All computer software, including PG, has bugs. PG currently lacks standardized verification and validation standards. There are well-established best practices, such as Institute of Electrical and Electronics Engineers (IEEE; 2017) Standard 1012, for verification and validation of software. (Matthews)

Trade secrecy: Software developers can withhold relevant information in criminal cases by citing trade secrecy protections. Evidence from PG software systems must be subject to robust adversarial scrutiny, and preventing trade secrets from blocking defense access is necessary to ensure fair and open criminal proceedings. (Wexler, Lynch, & Bradford)

SOURCE: Generated by the rapporteur based on workshop presentations from March 13 and 14, 2024.

---

for forensic DNA profiles. Understanding the results is a struggle not just for laypersons or attorneys, but also for analysts. Describing the results of PG requires using very specific language, and if the language is not used correctly, it can introduce subtle errors and biases. In addition, PG cannot overcome sample and profile limitations—a sample that is of poor quality and/or quantity cannot necessarily be rescued even by advanced tools like PG. Another limitation of PG, Rudin mentioned, is that no true value exists upon which to calibrate systems. That is, an expected likelihood ratio (the final output of PG) cannot be predicted (although an upper limit can be determined based on a single source profile). These limitations, she said, are insufficiently appreciated. Offering conclusions reached using PG about samples relevant to a crime event in court gives a "patina of science" that may lack a full understanding and description of the limitations, including sources of uncertainty and variability.

Uncertainty and Variation

Rudin identified two sources of uncertainty and variation that are extrinsic to PG—technological and human.

Rudin explained that the procedure for performing forensic DNA typing requires making multiple copies of particular DNA fragments in a sample so that sufficient material is available to analyze. This process, called *amplification*, is conceptually similar to making photocopies of a document. However, Rudin specified that if the same DNA sample is amplified multiple times (say, five times), the analyst may end up with five different results. She explained that this difference occurs due to random variations (called *stochastic sampling*) that can occur both before and during the amplification process. These variations can cause significant differences in the results ultimately obtained via PG, sometimes even more so than the differences you might see when using different PG programs, said Rudin.

Human factors, such as choosing the analytical threshold, can also have a significant impact on the results, continued Rudin. She explained that analytical thresholds can be based on validation studies but are generally implemented via policies that lack adequate accountability mechanisms. Importantly, Rudin noted, an analytical threshold is not selected or modeled by the software—rather, the threshold is determined by the laboratory or analyst based on lab protocols and policies before entering data into PG. The variance in analytical thresholds can affect the apparent number of contributors to the sample, as well as perceived missing information, and can affect the final PG result. Regardless of a technology's sophistication and power, said Rudin, "if you don't ask the right question, you won't get the right answer." The hypotheses that are posed are generally chosen by the laboratory, and the choice of those hypotheses is a significant factor in determining the final PG results. For example, are there assumed contributors to the sample, are there potentially concurrent contributors, and are there relatives involved? These factors can complicate the analysis and the hypotheses that are compared, she said, and can result in significantly different results. Sarah Chu, Perlmutter Center for Legal Justice at Cardozo Law, added that reducing variation and setting a standard of practice requires oversight and accountability systems. Jeanna Matthews, Clarkson University, pointed out that reducing variation is not the same thing as improving accuracy; variation can lead us to investigate why results differ and to seek out the correct answer.

Software Verification and Validation

Turning to considerations for implementation on the technological side of PG, Matthews reminded the audience that all computer software—including PG—has bugs. She emphasized that there are well-established best practices for verification and validation of software, and expressed concern that PG is not currently tested using these practices. Matthews explained that verification refers to whether the product was built correctly using the correct process, and validation refers to whether it was the right product that was built—that is, does the output meet the needs for which it was built? The well-established practices for building reliable software and iteratively identifying and removing defects include requirements definition, design definition, unit testing, integration testing, acceptance testing, regression testing, bug/defect tracking, version control, debuggers, and code coverage tools. Matthews noted that the U.S. government uses the IEEE (2017) Standard 1012 for System, Software, and Hardware Verification and Validation for critical software throughout the government, including software for aviation, at the National Aeronautics and Space Administration, and at the Nuclear Regulatory Commission (Box 3-4). The level of effort put into verification and validation, said Matthews, is guided by the integrity and severity level; for example, if the software impacts human life or liberty, the verification and validation process should be conducted at the highest level.

Ethics and Legality

Panelists also discussed ethical and legal concerns regarding the use of PG software by law enforcement. In this vein, Rudin noted that commercial PG programs present challenges to fair and equal access. Because the software itself is expensive and proprietary, it has not been possible to conduct true independent testing. Furthermore, she explained, independent experts face significant challenges in accessing the software to review casework, especially if the manufacturer considers them competitors. And, said Rudin, because people of color are overrepresented in the criminal justice system, they are disproportionately impacted by these limitations in access to commercial PG programs. She emphasized the need to identify options to provide equitable access for both research and casework.

Wexler agreed that lack of access is a major issue with PG. Specifically, she outlined how some software developers are currently able and incentivized to withhold relevant information entirely in a criminal case by citing trade secrecy protections. Wexler argued that instead of blocking defense access to PG entirely, trade secret privilege should merely provide a right to a reasonable protective order and, potentially, to courtroom closure. She noted that the United States is a "model to the world" in its commitment to fair and open criminal proceedings, which includes the right for the accused to confront witnesses against them and the obligation of prosecutors to disclose evidence to the defense. Wexler suggested that like all other

> **BOX 3-4**
> **IEEE Standard 1012 for System, Software, and Hardware Verification and Validation**
>
> The IEEE (2017) provides guidelines and requirements, via Standard 1012, for the verification and validation processes in the development of systems, software, and hardware. Below is an explanation of the key aspects of this standard:
>
> **Definition of Verification and Validation**
> *Verification*: The process of evaluating a system or component to determine whether the products of a given development phase satisfy the conditions imposed at the start of that phase.
> *Validation*: The process of evaluating a system or component during or at the end of the development process to determine whether it satisfies specified requirements.
>
> **Scope and Purpose**
> The standard's purpose is to establish a common framework for verification and validation processes, activities, and tasks to support all system, software, and hardware life cycle processes. It applies to systems, software, and hardware being developed, maintained, or reused (legacy, commercial off-the-shelf, etc.). It covers verification and validation processes for different integrity levels based on criticality analysis. Criticality analysis is used to identify mission-critical functions and components in a software system and involves an end-to-end functional decomposition performed by systems engineers. This systematic analysis covers the entire system, including hardware, software, and firmware components, which helps to prioritize verification and validation efforts and ensure that the most critical aspects of a system receive appropriate attention throughout the development process.

evidence, evidence from PG systems must be subject to robust adversarial scrutiny, and trade secrets should not be an exception to that requirement.

Considerations for Implementation

Expanding on her earlier discussion of trade secrets and protected information, Wexler pointed to the Justice in Forensics Algorithms Act (2024), a bill that has been introduced several times, and contains model language that would prevent trade secrets from being used to impede discovery of evidence: "There shall be no trade secret evidentiary privilege to withhold relevant evidence in criminal proceedings in the United States courts" (§ 2[b][1]). This language, said Wexler, could be used in a best practices guideline or as a requirement for procurement or federal grants. Inaccuracy and obstacles to transparency are an equity issue, said Wexler, due to the unfortunate reality that those accused of and victimized by crime

> **Verification and Validation Activities and Tasks**
> The standard defines a set of minimum required verification and validation tasks, as well as optional tasks that can be included based on project needs. Required tasks include requirements evaluation, design evaluation, implementation evaluation, test, and more. It provides guidance on planning, managing, measuring, monitoring, and reporting verification and validation efforts.
>
> **Life Cycle Processes**
> Verification and validation processes are integrated throughout the system/software/hardware life cycle. The standard covers activities such as concept documentation evaluation, disposal and retirement evaluation, and more. It supports different life cycle models, such as waterfall, incremental, and evolutionary.
>
> **Integrity Levels**
> The standard defines four integrity levels (1–4) based on criticality analysis of the system. Higher integrity levels require more stringent and comprehensive verification and validation efforts.
>
> **Evolution**
> IEEE 1012 has evolved over time, with major revisions in 1998, 2004, 2012, and 2016. The latest 2016 version aligns with other standards such as International Organization for Standardization (ISO)/International Electrotechnical Commission (IEC)/IEEE 15288 and ISO/IEC 12207. In summary, IEEE 1012 provides a framework for planning, executing, and managing verification and validation processes throughout the life cycle of systems, software, and hardware projects to ensure they meet specified requirements and intended use.
>
> SOURCE: Generated by the rapporteur based on IEEE, 2017.

are disproportionately from poor communities and communities of color. Wexler noted that the criminal legal system relies conceptually on equally matched adversaries with a neutral fact finder, but when there are unnecessary impediments to one side doing their job, it skews the ability of the system to reach accurate outcomes.

Wexler echoed the conclusions of the National Institute of Standards and Technology and the Government Accountability Office that PG should be subject to review by independent researchers who have no stake in the outcome. Unfortunately, she noted, many vendors refuse to allow this type of access. Wexler shared that she and her colleagues in computer science, law, and forensic genealogy put together a team to conduct a review of PG. However, when they reached out to companies to purchase a research license, they were ultimately denied, with one reporting that they do not provide research licenses. Rudin said that she is "mystified to some extent" by the reluctance of developers to have independent groups confirm the software. For programs that are, in fact, accurate and reliable, independent confirmation would reassure all interested parties.

Under the *Daubert* standard, which is used to determine admissibility of evidence (*Daubert v. Merrell Dow Pharmaceuticals, Inc.*, 1993), judges consider whether the method used to generate scientific evidence has been subjected to publication and peer review and accepted within the relevant scientific community, said Wexler. Representatives of PG companies have testified under oath that their product is subject to peer review, she said, and that the results should therefore be admissible. However, they do not allow independent research into quality assurance and validation. Matthews added that the "relevant scientific community" does not usually include software engineering, despite the fact that the evidence in question was generated by software.

Bille highlighted the importance of establishing standards and regulations for PG. He mentioned the need for validation of PG software to ensure its reliability and accuracy by the laboratories. Bille also discussed the role of organizations such as SWGDAM, Organization of Scientific Area Committees, the UK Forensic Science Regulator, and the DNA Commission of the International Society for Forensic Genetics in developing standards for the validation and use of PG. In addition, forensic laboratories that participate in the Combined DNA Index System (CODIS) must comply with the National Quality Assurance Standards and accredited labs must comply with the standards of their accrediting body such as the American National Standards Institute's National Accreditation Board. Wexler asserted that vendors of PG should be required to allow independent audits, and procurement guidelines for law enforcement should include a requirement that the tools are subject to independent peer review from people with no stake in the outcome. Matthews emphasized that it is not "too late to get this right in the DNA space." Software will continue to be developed and implemented within the criminal legal system, and she suggested that rather than continue operating without consistent standards, the field should require that software engineering best practices be followed and push back against trade secrets protections being used as a shield to refuse disclosure of evidence. Public trust requires transparency and accountability, said Matthews, and we need to make the necessary changes now to set a course for future technologies.

REFLECTIONS

Following panelist presentations, Chu, serving as discussant, offered her reflections and perspective on the topics discussed. When forensic DNA analysis was first developed, she noted, there were many difficult conversations about the associated ethical, legal, social, and justice issues. As DNA analysis become more ubiquitous and less expensive, these conversations, questions, and critiques largely fell away. Now there is an explosion in technologies, she said, that has left the public and decision-makers struggling to catch up with ethical, social, and justice implications. Chu suggested that while PG has potential to assist in criminal investigations, there is a need to carefully consider these implications and to ensure that the technology is reliable and useful. Getting it right is important for everyone's sake, she said, but particularly for historically overpoliced communities of color, where the harms of these new technologies are concentrated.

"What do we owe each other when we are implementing PG systems?" posed Chu. She suggested that justice and transparency require robust and comprehensive validation studies and standards that are not restricted by commercial restraints or adversarial legal systems, as well as use of PG that is data driven rather than politically driven. Validation is integral to generating reliable results, the conclusions we can draw from the results, and how much confidence we have in the results. Chu emphasized the need for federal support to help laboratories conduct validation studies and to make the data publicly available, noting that most labs lack the infrastructure and resources to maintain databases to share information. Centralized databases supported by the federal government could thus play a key role in improving transparency. Chu identified another important role for the federal government—as well as state and local entities—in conditioning grants and procurement on requirements that software be developed under IEEE Standard 1012 (2017) and that software be made accessible and available to both researchers and defendants. Furthermore, labs should disclose their PG records so that defense attorneys can review the assumptions and choices that underlie the results presented in court. If we permit technology companies to use trade secrets arguments to avoid sharing PG evidence, said Chu, there is a risk that as the role of technologies in the criminal legal system expands, more and more evidence will be withheld. This would make it impossible to have a "fair and just system," she said.

Finally, Chu suggested, decisions about the use of forensic DNA technologies need to be driven by data rather than politics. As an example of this problem, Chu said that laboratories across the country have been told by law enforcement and political leaders that they should swab every gun for genetic material. These swabs tend to produce low quantity, high contributor mixtures which are among the hardest samples to interpret through PG. Limited law enforcement resources, she suggested, could instead be used to process higher-yield cases and use sexual assault kits, for example. In addition, results from gun swabs generally cannot be entered into CODIS, so these tests incentivize the growth of local DNA databases that are not required to follow state regulations. Testing policies should be determined in conjunction with forensic scientists and other stakeholders, said Chu, calling for open, transparent discussions among experts and members of the public about DNA collection, retention, and expungement policies. Chu suggested that taking these steps will help ensure that law enforcement does not become overly reliant on technology and the type of DNA collection practices that can erode trust in law enforcement.

4

Forensic DNA Phenotyping

OVERVIEW OF FORENSIC DNA PHENOTYPING (FDP)

Alicia Carriquiry, Iowa State University and chair of the workshop planning committee, moderated this session of the workshop, which focused on FDP (see Box 4-1). The panel featured speakers with expertise in biology, biotechnology, anthropology, and criminal legal defense reform. The session examined the potential of FDP to function as an investigative tool while also emphasizing the significant ethical, legal, and social challenges associated with its use. Several participants called for careful consideration of these issues to ensure that FDP is used responsibly and effectively in the criminal legal system.

Presentations began with Susan Walsh, Indiana University Indianapolis, who explained that FDP is used to infer likely phenotypic characteristics (such as eye, hair, and skin color) from DNA left at crime scenes. It is intended to provide investigative leads by predicting physical traits of unknown persons of interest based on their genetic material.

Walsh provided an overview of the different types of professionals that work on FDP. Researchers focus on identifying variants or genes that are associated with human traits and generally focus on appearance, age, or ancestry. Commercial partners develop tools that allow laboratories to use the information generated by the researchers. Many work with researchers and use the markers and models that researchers have provided, although others use their own methods. The public, said Walsh, tend to have a narrow view of FDP through "big splash news stories" that highlight specific cases.

BOX 4-1
Overview of Forensic DNA Phenotyping

The following overview reflects information shared in presentations from multiple workshop speakers. They should not be construed as consensus or exhaustive definitions of the topics discussed.

What is it? *Forensic DNA phenotyping* (FDP)* is a technique that aims to predict visible physical characteristics and biogeographical ancestry of an unknown person from DNA evidence left at a crime scene, typically used for investigative lead generation. It is an investigative intelligence tool that provides information about likely physical traits from DNA to help inform or narrow a police investigation, rather than a means of definitive identification like traditional DNA profiling.

How does it work? FDP involves analyzing specific regions of DNA and applying predictive modeling to infer traits such as eye, hair, and skin color; age; facial features; and the geographic ancestry or ethnic background of a sample's source. This is done by looking at how certain genes influence the expression of these visible characteristics. The goal is to generate investigative leads about the unidentified person's appearance and origins when there is no match in criminal DNA databases. The predicted traits can then be used to focus the investigation on potential suspects, missing persons, or unidentified human remains.

Who is involved in its use? Generally, law enforcement agencies contract with private consultants and/or external vendors that offer FDP services and tools.

What is the scale of use? FDP is an emerging technique with increasing commercial availability. Though there are examples of its use by forensic laboratories in the United States, it has not been widely adopted. FDP is typically used for investigative lead generation rather than routine casework.

What regulations and/or guidelines apply to its use? In the United States, there is currently no federal law regulating FDP specifically, and most states do not have laws addressing FDP specifically.** The Federal Bureau of Investigation's Quality Assurance Standards, which became effective as of July 2020, provide guidelines for forensic DNA testing laboratories. While not mentioning FDP specifically, they cover validation requirements for new methodologies used in DNA analysis.

---

*The DNA technologies discussed at the workshop are not referred to with consistent terminology by forensic, law enforcement, and legal experts, with multiple variations on the names of the technologies discussed at this workshop. For consistency, the terms *forensic investigative genetic genealogy*, *probabilistic genotyping software*, and *forensic DNA phenotyping* are used across these workshop proceedings.

**Some states are considering new legislation to regulate FDP. For example, New York state legislators proposed Bill S. 226, "An Act to amend the executive law, in relation to prohibiting the use of DNA phenotyping in criminal prosecutions and proceedings."

SOURCE: Definitions presented by Heather McKiernan and Craig O'Connor on March 13, 2024. Regulations and guidelines sourced from workshop discussions and presentations on March 13 and 14, 2024.

Looking for variants or genes associated with a trait is like looking for a "needle in a haystack," said Walsh. Traits may be binary, categorical, or continuous, and the variants or genes can be highly or only slightly associated with the traits. Once relevant genes or variants are identified, they are combined to create a reliable tool that can be used for prediction. Walsh said that the data, methods, and models created by researchers in this field are published and peer reviewed. She emphasized that the process of FDP is designed to accumulate intelligence about persons of interest, not to identify a single suspect; the intelligence generated by FDP must be followed by normal police work to investigate further.

FDP predictions are group based, not individual, said Walsh. This means that the results will provide likelihood information on multiple traits and will highlight several potential phenotypes of interest. Rather than producing a single definitive prediction of an individual based on DNA, FDP provides information about the likelihood of several traits. Later, Walsh noted that in her scientific opinion, it is currently not possible to reliably predict facial morphology through FDP. She noted that facial morphology prediction could be possible in the future, and that she is working with other scientists to deepen understanding of the genetic formation of the face. For now, she reiterated, FDP does not enable law enforcement to point to a single individual but can inform police investigations.

Walsh explained the current state of evidence in appearance, age, and ancestry prediction. Associations are described with an area under the curve (AUC) metric that represents predictive value; an AUC of 1 would be a perfect prediction and an AUC of 0.5 would be comparable to "tossing a coin." Predictions of brown and blue eye color are fairly accurate, with AUCs of 0.95 and 0.94. Hair and skin color predictions are slightly less accurate, with AUCs ranging from 0.72 for brown hair to 0.92 for red hair and 0.72 for pale skin and 0.96 for dark-to-black skin. Walsh stressed that while some of these predictions are fairly reliable, all of them will produce some false positives and false negatives. Other traits associated with a predictive gene or variant include eyebrow color, freckling, hair shape, and baldness. There is no DNA model available for continuous height prediction, given that hundreds of thousands of markers would be needed, and many environmental factors contribute to an individual's height. The process for predicting age is slightly different and involves detecting and measuring methylated DNA regions; this process results in a quantitative output.

Ancestry prediction uses genetic data to infer the geographic origin of the person's most recent ancestors, said Walsh. It can be conducted using select ancestry informative markers or large-scale genetic data, but the prediction is only as good as the reference population. Walsh stressed that ancestry prediction should not be used to predict a phenotype and vice versa. Each assessment should be considered an independent test that helps accumulate information toward a fuller representation of the sample tested.

Walsh provided an example of the types of predictions that result from FDP analysis. She explained that currently, biologists can provide prediction results of the most probable physical traits associated with a DNA sample, for a discrete set of traits. While a most probable presentation of a trait (such as blue eyes) is indicated by the results, there is still a real possibility that the most probable presentation is not the actual presentation. Walsh noted that epistasis and epigenetics, fields where knowledge is actively evolving, can affect the expression of genes.

The results of FDP can also be translated into a possible visual interpretation, Walsh explained. Given the potential variability of traits, and the independent nature of each trait, Walsh noted that the most accurate visual representation of FDP results based on current science would include multiple images that offer simple visual indicators for discrete traits such as eye or hair color, hair texture, presence of balding, skin tone, presence of freckles, eyebrow color, and age prediction (see Figure 4-1).

Walsh concluded by emphasizing her views on the need for independent validation and peer review of genetic phenotyping tools used by law enforcement, both of the underlying science and of products of FDP, including the best practices for presentation of results. During the Q&A session, an audience participant noted that in addition, independent validation of software as it is deployed in the field is necessary to ensure reliable and accurate use of such technology.

CONSIDERATIONS FOR FDP USE BY LAW ENFORCEMENT

Opportunities

Asked to consider opportunities around law enforcement use of FDP (see Box 4-2), Walsh explained that for unsolved cases in which other investigative leads have gone cold, FDP can be used as part of normal police work to accumulate intelligence that may help narrow down a list of suspects or help generate leads in identifying a missing person. She explained that unlike traditional testing that compares a sample from a crime scene to a potential suspect, FDP generates information about what an individual may look like based on their genetic profile and can thus be a unique tool for lead generation. Walsh clarified that as an investigative tool, FDP intelligence is then followed by normal police work to investigate further.

These uses echoed those highlighted by Paul Belli, International Homicide Investigators Association, and Leigh Clark, Florida Department of Law Enforcement, in the law enforcement perspectives panel (see Chapter 1). Belli and Clark described previous examples of FDP use as a means of

Prediction Result Example using current scientific knowledge

Probability Estimates & Verbal Description – MALE PROFILE (STR KNOWLEDGE)

Blue 0.93 Intermediate 0.02 Brown 0.05
Most probable eye color is Blue

Blond 0.03 Brown 0.31 Black 0.65 Red 0.01; Shade: Dark 0.93
Most probable hair color Dark Brown/Black

Straight Hair Yes 0.8 No 0.2
Straight hair is the most probably prediction

Balding Yes 0.1 No 0.9
Absence of balding is the most probable prediction

Very Pale 0.1 Pale 0.5 Intermediate 0.33 Dark 0.06 Dark-Black 0.01
Most probable skin color Pale to Intermediate

Freckles Yes 0.3 No 0.7
Absence of freckling is the most probable prediction

Blond 0.05 Brown 0.4 Black 0.55
Most probable eyebrow color Black to Dark Brown

Age Prediction from blood sample 26±3.2 years
Most probable age range predicted 20-30 years old.

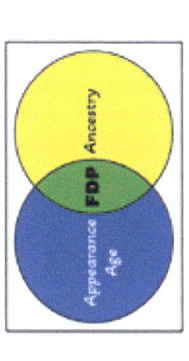

VISUAL INTERPRETATION OF VERBAL
SUBJECTIVE

Ancestry proportions*
European 0.6
North African 0.2
Sub Saharan African 0.01
East Asian 0.12
South/Central Asia 0.05
Middle East 0.02

**Should not reflect the phenotype prediction*

FIGURE 4-1 Examples of forensic DNA phenotyping (FDP) prediction result using current scientific knowledge.
SOURCE: Presented by Susan Walsh on March 14, 2024.

BOX 4-2
Opportunities and Challenges in Using FDP Identified by Workshop Speakers

Opportunities

Technological capabilities: FDP can generate predictions about an individual's appearance based on their genetic profile, including hair color, skin pigmentation, freckling, and eye color. Emerging markers aim to predict body height and refine geographic ancestry. (Walsh)

Generating leads: FDP can be used in an investigative capacity for unsolved cases where other leads have gone cold, helping to generate leads, inform investigation priorities, narrow down suspects or find missing persons. (Walsh)

Challenges

Consistency and objectivity: The use and interpretation of FDP results by law enforcement can be influenced by human factors such as implicit bias, confirmation bias, and tunnel vision. Additionally, because FDP is often used as a last resort in attempts to generate leads, there can be limited evidence to independently corroborate predictions. (Brown)

Disparate impact: Because communities of color are overrepresented in the criminal legal system, any risks associated with the use of advanced forensic DNA technologies affect communities of color disproportionately. Insofar as it produces visual representations, FDP has risks similar to those associated with traditional police sketches, including racial profiling or misidentification, potentially leading to innocent people becoming the focus of investigations. (Brown & Martschenko)

Limitations of current science: There may be a gap between what the public believes is possible in the case of FDP and what the current science enables. It is important for the implementation of FDP for law enforcement investigative use to be independently validated and openly peer reviewed, hallmarks of the scientific enterprise. (Walsh & Martschenko)

SOURCE: Generated by the rapporteur based on workshop presentations from March 13 and 14, 2024.

generating investigative leads in the absence of other evidence for the identification of both suspects and of unidentified human remains, and as a tool for garnering renewed public attention for a case.

Challenges and Ethical Considerations

Uncertainty and Scope of Impact

Rebecca Brown, Maat Strategies, framed her presentation in terms of considerations related to law enforcement applications of FDP in the field, including questions around the potential for accuracy to be impacted when a tool moves from laboratory to field use, how relative accuracy can be misunderstood by law enforcement, and the need to carefully evaluate the utility of investing limited criminal justice resources in the use of FDP. Without careful regulation of investigative tools, suggested Brown, innocent people can inadvertently become the focus of investigations. She expressed the view that these applications' relative value to crime solving may not outweigh potential risk to the public good. Brown pointed to an example of National Institute of Standards and Technology tests of facial recognition algorithms in nonlab settings, which found that accuracy rates varied widely between demographic groups, with certain racial demographics seeing higher rates of misidentification. She called for FDP models to undergo similar independent forensic validation to assess their accuracy on samples derived from real-world case studies, under the supervision of institutional review boards. Brown also suggested that in moving from the lab to real-world application, analysts should also account for environmental factors that influence appearance, such as body choices including diet, cosmetic surgery, makeup, or hair dye. To this point, Walsh and O'Connor both noted in previous presentations the extent to which genetic markers may vary from phenotypical presentation—particularly around racial identity. FDP involves probabilistic inferences, said Brown, which invite human factors, such as confirmation bias, implicit bias, and tunnel vision, to impact how the information is used. Brown expressed her concern that FDP application may be more prone to impact by problematic human factors. For example, law enforcement officers may exhibit confirmation bias and interpret FDP-generated information in ways that confirm their existing beliefs or may focus only on the direction suggested by FDP while ignoring other leads. Brown also noted an example where law enforcement use of FDP had previously enabled racial profiling. In that case, genetic evidence suggested that a Black person had committed a crime; police used this information to obtain DNA swabs from hundreds of Black and Hispanic men who had previously been arrested in the general area of the crime.

Brown noted that there are multiple examples of investigative tools being expanded beyond their original intended use. For example, color-based field drug tests were developed as a preliminary testing method; results were to be confirmed by laboratory testing. However, despite evidence about unreliability and even warnings from the vendors of the tests, these tests remain in use and are responsible for hundreds of thousands of arrests each year. Echoing Bradford in the earlier ethics panel, Brown emphasized the significant impact a false arrest can have on an individual's life. It is essential, she suggested, that we carefully weigh the use of law enforcement technologies with the cumulative costs and harms to society. She urged the audience to ask themselves, "If the goal before us is to identify those tools best equipped to solve crime, given limited resources and our inability to control the psychological factors impacting investigations like tunnel vision and implicit bias, should this particular tool be employed?"

Understanding and Education

Brown offered her view of the potential risks related to law enforcement use of visual representations of suspects, particularly given the biases inherent in eyewitness and public response to these images. One of the most unreliable procedures used by law enforcement to identify a suspect is the traditional composite sketch, she explained. Innocent people have been arrested because they share resemblance to a composite. In addition, Brown explained that memory is malleable and can be altered through the viewing of a composite, leading to an inability to properly identify the actual perpetrator later. Finally, cross-racial misidentification is a common issue in wrongful convictions. Brown also noted her concern that the public may misperceive FDP-generated images as definitive images of a suspect rather than as an investigative tool.

In a previous panel featuring law enforcement perspectives, speakers noted that FDP is often used when other traditional forms of investigation have been unable to generate leads. Brown reiterated this point, noting that use of FDP in this context can mean there is little to no evidence to independently corroborate a phenotyping prediction or public identification of a suspect based on a phenotyping prediction.

"We cannot train our way out of the shortcomings of these tools," said Brown. Implicit bias, confirmation bias, and tunnel vision are human factors that impact the way an FDP result is interpreted by law enforcement and members of the public.

Disparate Impact

The risks of FDP and other forensic DNA technologies fall disproportionately on communities of color, said Brown, pointing to existing evidence of racial profiling and DNA dragnets, and noting that these consequences can extend to wrongful arrest and conviction. Brown explained that there is the additional risk of reinforcing racial biases and stigmatizing certain populations.

Brown suggested that if law enforcement relies on FDP or other advanced forensic DNA technologies to the detriment of the communities they serve, trust will be eroded. Furthermore, relying on advanced forensic DNA technologies can waste resources that could be directed elsewhere. For example, there are thousands of untested rape kits, and thousands of drug arrests predicated on color-based drug tests. Brown suggested that investing in using validated tools in these areas would be a better use of limited resources.

CONSIDERATIONS FOR IMPLEMENTATION

The presenters next discussed considerations for implementation.

Ethical Considerations

Matthias Wienroth, Northumbria University, offered an accounting of the state of the art of forensic science in terms of its engagement with ethics. Wienroth noted that both forensic analysts and law enforcement officials typically associate their roles with a moral duty to protect the public from harm. This is complicated, he noted, by the fact that this duty can come into direct conflict with other values, including fairness, equity, and public trust. Wienroth encouraged the audience to carefully consider efforts to weigh the risks and benefits of implementing advanced genetic forensic technologies, and to recognize that even in those cases where a technology leads to the resolution of the case, there can be significant costs.

Before continuing with the implementation of advanced genetic forensic technologies, Wienroth said that the public needs to ask several questions. Are laboratories capable of employing the statistical and probabilistic methods required to apply these approaches? Are service providers ready to discuss and address the limitations of technologies as well as challenges of application by forensic scientists and law enforcement officials in real-world settings? Are law enforcement processes prepared for reliably, usefully, and legitimately integrating new and emerging forensic genetics technologies into the practice of law enforcement and investigation? Are advanced forensic DNA technology practitioners working transparently? Are they aware of the societal context in which they operate and what that means for their own practice? In moving forward, Wienroth suggested, we should consider ethics in law enforcement use of advanced forensic DNA technologies not as a hurdle that must be cleared, but as an embedded, everyday practice.

Frameworks for Governance and Oversight

To meaningfully implement this kind of ethics, Wienroth suggested, requires enforceable self-governance, with enforcement mechanisms that are both internal and external to the field. Wienroth proposed a framework for the ethical implementation of FDP that considers reliability, utility, and legitimacy (Figure 4-2). This framework emphasizes the need for reliable scientific methods, useful applications that genuinely aid investigations, and legitimate practices that are transparent and inclusive. Wienroth explained that this framework relies on effective governance structures, including independent validation and public reporting, which he said are necessary for overseeing the use of FDP.

Other speakers echoed Wienroth's calls for governance and oversight and reemphasized the importance of public education and transparency around the use of advanced forensic DNA technologies. Walsh outlined methods for enhancing transparency and accuracy in law enforcement use of FDP. Specifically, she highlighted the need for peer-reviewed publications on the science behind the tool, prediction model design, and performance of the predictions on global independent test sets. She also identified a need for guidelines on how to understand and report results from FDP, and for education and training for users of the tool, law enforcement, and the public. Finally, Walsh called for standardized, publicly available sample sets to

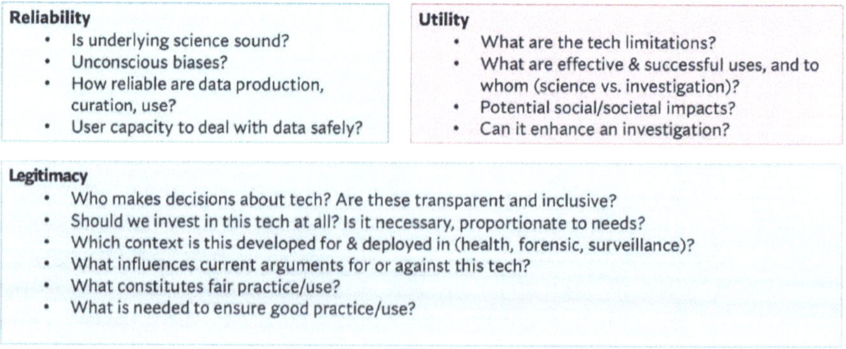

Reliability	Utility
• Is underlying science sound? • Unconscious biases? • How reliable are data production, curation, use? • User capacity to deal with data safely?	• What are the tech limitations? • What are effective & successful uses, and to whom (science vs. investigation)? • Potential social/societal impacts? • Can it enhance an investigation?

Legitimacy
- Who makes decisions about tech? Are these transparent and inclusive?
- Should we invest in this tech at all? Is it necessary, proportionate to needs?
- Which context is this developed for & deployed in (health, forensic, surveillance)?
- What influences current arguments for or against this tech?
- What constitutes fair practice/use?
- What is needed to ensure good practice/use?

FIGURE 4-2 Reliability, utility, and legitimacy framework for the ethical implementation of forensic DNA phenotyping.
SOURCE: Presented by Matthias Wienroth on March 14, 2024.

examine both the science of the method and the impact of result interpretation by law enforcement.

REFLECTIONS

Following the panelist presentations, Daphne Martschenko, Stanford University, offered her reflections. This panel discussion, she said, emphasized the importance of being very clear about terminology. Brown demonstrated the differences in how "accuracy" is understood in the laboratory, in real-world cases, and by the public. Wienroth identified reliability, utility, and legitimacy as important concepts, said Martschenko, but what do these terms mean to different actors? Who gets to determine what these terms mean? Martschenko emphasized that workshop discussions had made clear that problems arise when independent parties do not have the opportunity to inform decisions about what is reliable, beneficial, or legitimate. Reconciling the different understandings of the concepts in forensic DNA technologies may require educating the public, the media, and researchers about how technologies are used and understood downstream. Ultimately, "these tools should not be made available to those who do not have the training to use them or the education to know how to appropriately interpret findings," said Martschenko.

The public release of FDP-generated images has the potential to bring groups of people under suspicion, and existing biases may be reinforced within the legal system. There is a fraught relationship between race and genetic ancestry, and describing race as biological rather than as a sociopolitical construct can have very harmful consequences, she said. Despite researchers' best intentions, FDP predictions are often misunderstood as identifying specific individuals.

Multiple speakers at the workshop have emphasized the need for an agreed-upon threshold for scientific accuracy prior to implementation of technologies, as well as the need for independent verification, professional and ethical guidelines, and oversight and governance, said Martschenko. She said that while all of these are critically important, we need to be comfortable revisiting and adjusting the needs as technologies are implemented and evaluated. Furthermore, there is a need to answer fundamental questions about who defines the risks and benefits, and for whom justice is being served through the use of advanced forensic DNA technologies. If we do not address these issues, she said, "we create an environment that's ripe for unaccountability, for ambiguity, and for mistrust."

5

Learning from Abroad

In this workshop session, moderated by Natalie Ram, University of Maryland King Carey School of Law, presenters provided perspective on law enforcement use of emerging forensic DNA technologies abroad. Presenters included individuals from Australia, Portugal, the United Kingdom, and Switzerland with expertise in forensic genetics, biochemical engineering, sociology, law, criminal justice, and forensic medicine and molecular biology. Their presentations highlighted the diverse approaches to regulation and use of advanced forensic DNA technologies by law enforcement across the United Kingdom, Europe, and Australia.

BEST PRACTICES AMID A REGULATORY VACUUM IN AUSTRALIA

Dennis McNevin, University of Technology Sydney, began the session by describing the status of each of the advanced forensic DNA technologies in Australia. He started with probabilistic genotyping (PG), noting that many speakers had emphasized the importance of testing PG for accuracy and reliability. McNevin said that he is not aware of any interlaboratory comparisons of PG results among forensic laboratories in Australia; one lab participated in an external proficiency test, but the results are not publicly available. He noted that developers of PG have argued against interlaboratory comparisons because of differences in human factors, lab policies, and other elements extrinsic to the software. McNevin said that it is reasonable to expect that results should be comparable across labs, and that comparisons can account for interlaboratory differences (McNevin et al., 2021).[1]

Forensic DNA phenotyping (FDP) for externally visible characteristics is used in Australia, said McNevin, as is testing for inference of biographical ancestry (BGA). He said that in his view, BGA should not be considered a type of FDP. He explained that phenotyping refers to an essential quality of an individual as a result of their DNA, whereas ancestry estimation indicates where an individual's ancestors may have come from but does not reveal any "essential characteristic" of the individual. McNevin noted that Australian law enforcement currently uses FDP only to infer eye and hair color, and not to infer skin color or other externally visible traits. McNevin noted that in Australia, FDP and BGA are typically employed only if other testing—such as short tandem repeat (STR) direct matching and familial searching—fails to confirm an identity. In addition, privacy impact assessments are now typically conducted before implementing FDP or BGA (Box 5-1). McNevin said that in his opinion, phenotypes and ancestry inferences should be retained in house for investigative purposes and not released to the public in order to avoid possible stigmatization of certain communities. Describing the legal context, McNevin explained that there is a legislative vacuum for both FDP and BGA in Australia; neither is explicitly allowed or disallowed.

There is also a legislative vacuum around forensic investigative genetic genealogy (FIGG), said McNevin. As a result, FIGG operates under a privacy umbrella (e.g., Commonwealth Privacy Act, 1988, and amendments). Under these regulations, FIGG is subject to regulatory aspects designed to ensure ethical and transparent use (Box 5-2). McNevin also noted that the use of privacy impact assessments is widespread in Australian law enforcement and is an integral part of FIGG implementation.

McNevin explained the process of implementing FIGG in cases of missing persons as part of a framework of sequential unmasking of information. Cases begin with testing autosomal STRs and uploading the profile to the National Criminal Identification DNA Database (NCIDD). If there is no hit, the profile would be uploaded to the familial searching extension of NCIDD, and next a Y-chromosome STR (Y-STR) or mitochondrial DNA profile could be uploaded to the same database to look for maternal or paternal relatives. If there are no meaningful leads after these steps, the STR profile could be uploaded to the International Criminal Police Organization

---

[1] As McNevin described, this comparison method involves applying PG to a dilution series of a DNA mixture to determine where the likelihood ratio plateaus. Because different laboratories use different assays with different loci, this method includes only loci that are common among all participating labs. In addition, each lab uses the same population allele frequencies and subpopulation correction factor theta. With this method, said McNevin, interlaboratory comparisons are possible.

> **BOX 5-1**
> **Best Practices for Privacy Impact Assessments**
>
> The Office of the Australian Information Commissioner defines a *privacy impact assessment* (PIA) as a systematic assessment of a project that identifies potential privacy impacts and recommendations to manage, minimize, or eliminate them (Australian Federal Police, 2023). Australian government agencies are mandated to conduct a PIA for all high-privacy-risk projects. To be effective, a privacy impact assessment should be integrated into the project planning process seamlessly. This integration facilitates a privacy-by-design approach and identifies best practices, outlined below:
>
> **Integrate PIAs into project planning:** Ensure that PIAs are an integral part of the project planning process to facilitate a privacy-by-design approach.
>
> **Identify better practices:** Use privacy impact assessments to identify and implement better privacy practices within the project.
>
> **Ensure compliance with the Privacy Act:** Conduct privacy impact assessments to help ensure that the project complies with the Privacy Act and other relevant privacy regulations.
>
> **Mandatory for high-privacy-risk projects:** Australian government agencies are required to undertake a privacy impact assessment for all high-privacy-risk projects.
>
> **Education and training:** Engage in educational resources, such as the Office of the Australian Information Commissioner's free e-learning course on conducting privacy impact assessments, to improve understanding and execution of privacy impact assessments.
>
> SOURCE: Adapted from *Guide to undertaking a privacy impact assessment* (Office of the Australian Commissioner, 2021): https://www.oaic.gov.au/privacy/privacy-guidance-for-organisations-and-government-agencies/privacy-impact-assessments/guide-to-undertaking-privacy-impact-assessments

(INTERPOL) DNA database, and then to I-FAMILIA (INTERPOL Family Associated Matching to Identify Lost Individuals Abroad). Following this, Y-STRs and mitochondrial DNA could be searched in I-FAMILIA, and then Y-STRs would be searched using the Y-STR Haplotype Reference Database and mitochondrial DNA to the EMPOP Database.[2] Finally, said McNevin, if all of these steps failed to generate a meaningful lead, a single nucleotide

---

[2] EMPOP stands for the European DNA Profiling Group mtDNA Population (Database).

BOX 5-2
Australian Regulations on FIGG

Specific legislation directly addressing FIGG is not well established in Australia. In the absence of specific FIGG legislation, privacy laws such as the Commonwealth Privacy Act (1988) have been applied to regulate the use of genetic information in forensic contexts. Under this existing framework:

Legal and ethical oversight: FIGG use must be approved by a governance board comprising legal, scientific, and investigative advisors. This board ensures that cases meet strict criteria before FIGG can be employed. The privacy impact assessment process (see Box 5-1) is integral to FIGG implementation, involving wide engagement with stakeholders to ensure the safe and transparent use of the technique (Australian Federal Police, 2023; New South Wales [NSW] Police Force, n.d.).

Case criteria: FIGG is used only for identifying unknown human remains or perpetrators of serious violent crimes, such as homicides and sexual assaults. All other routine investigative and DNA analysis techniques must be exhausted, or there must be a serious and immediate threat to public safety before FIGG is considered (NSW Police Force, n.d.).

Database use and consent: Only two consumer DNA databases, GEDmatch PRO and FamilyTreeDNA, are authorized for law enforcement use of FIGG. These databases contain profiles of individuals who have consented to law enforcement searches. According to the NSW Police Force, Australians make up an estimated 5%–10% of the profiles on these databases (NSW Police Force, n.d.; Wakelin & Mendes, 2023).

Data management: DNA profiles must be removed from all databases upon case closure. Regular reviews of the policy and use of FIGG in casework are mandated to ensure ongoing compliance and ethical standards (NSW Police Force, n.d.).

Privacy and ethical considerations: The use of FIGG must comply with the Privacy Act and other relevant privacy regulations. The information privacy principles apply to DNA profiles held by forensic laboratories and stored on databases, ensuring the confidentiality and security of personal information (Australian Federal Police, 2023; Australian Law Reform Commission, 2010).

SOURCE: Generated by the rapporteur, based on a presentation by Dennis McNiven on March 14, 2023.

polymorphism (SNP) profile would be generated in order to undertake the process of FIGG (see Figure 5-1).

It is essential, said McNevin, to educate and "bring the public along" in the use of FIGG. The Australian Federal Police DNA Program for Unidentified and Missing Persons engages with the public through its website, which provides information to families of missing persons as well as members of the public who may wish to contribute DNA to assist in identifying missing persons.

TENTATIVE USE OF FIGG IN EUROPE

Rafaela Granja, University of Minho, focused her remarks on the use of FIGG across Europe and the unique nature of the professional origins of FIGG. She reported growing interest in FIGG in Europe, although it is still in very early stages. Granja explained that Sweden recently used FIGG for the first time to solve a double-murder cold case that occurred in 2004. Since Swedish law does not specifically allow the use of genetic information for FIGG, the Swedish Authority for Privacy Protection has blocked further use of the technology until the law is changed. Granja explained that the Biometrics and Forensics Ethics Group in the United Kingdom stated that the preliminary use of FIGG in the identification of unidentifiable human bodies would allow its potential to be tested. However, she continued, the agency has raised concerns about the adequacy of traditional informed

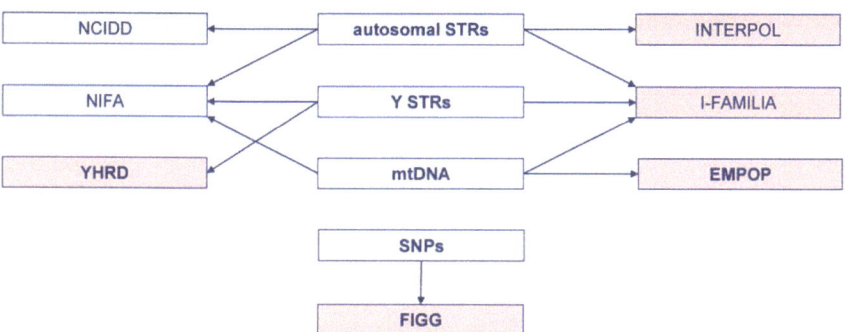

FIGURE 5-1 Sequential unmasking of information before using forensic investigative genetic genealogy (FIGG).
NOTE: EMPOP = EDNAP (European DNA Profiling Group) mtDNA Population Database; I-FAMILIA = INTERPOL Family Associated Matching to Identify Lost Individuals Abroad; INTERPOL = International Criminal Police Organization; mtDNA = mitochondrial DNA; NCIDD = National Criminal Identification DNA Database; NIFA = Network Intrusion Forensics Analyst; SNP = single nucleotide polymorphism; STR = short tandem repeat; YHRD = Y-STR Haplotype Reference Database.
SOURCE: Presented by Dennis McNevin on March 14, 2024.

consent in the context of FIGG and has highlighted the need to reconsider traditional notions of informed consent to ensure ethical and responsible use of genetic data in forensic investigations. This concern about traditional conceptions of informed consent echoed concerns expressed during the workshop discussion of PG.

While FIGG gained traction after the Golden State Killer investigation, said Granja, the story of FIGG has longer roots. People have been engaging in genetic genealogy as a hobby for many years, and this field of expertise has emerged as a form of "citizen science." Early on, this often took the form of law enforcement agencies and citizen genealogists working together to solve missing persons cases. This partnership, she said, means that hobbyists with diverse backgrounds have become a source of expertise for criminal investigations. It is "of paramount importance" that this community's involvement with the criminal justice system is formalized and that safeguards are put in place. These safeguards could include accreditation or regulatory procedures that limit who can play a role in this system. Current safeguards, she said, are largely self-regulatory efforts; instead of self-regulation, there is a need for a diverse group of stakeholders to make decisions about the complex issues involved with FIGG. FIGG has largely been shielded from public criticism by the perception that it is used to increase public safety and provide healing for victims, said Granja. However, law enforcement use of recreational DNA databases is an example of "function creep," with implications for civil liberties. FIGG and other forensic DNA technologies are social issues with social implications, she said, and privacy needs to be considered a social value.

A LACK OF CLARITY IN ENGLAND AND WALES

Carole McCartney, University of Leicester Law School, told workshop participants about the use of forensic DNA technologies in England and Wales. It is an entirely private forensic science marketplace, she said, with the police contracting with one of the three large providers. The commercial nature of the marketplace for DNA testing means that the contracts between the police and the providers dictate which technologies are available and complicate the issue of transparency. It is not a healthy marketplace, she said; there is enormous financial pressure on the companies to sell their technologies, and prices have been forced down by the risk of company failure when providers must compete, as well as by cuts to police budgets. The government has not stepped in with a strategic plan for advanced forensic DNA technologies, said McCartney; the last U.K. Home Office (2018) document, *Biometrics Strategy: Better Public Services Maintaining Public Trust*, contained a paucity of detail and no underlying principles of future strategy on forensic DNA.

In gauging the current use of advanced DNA technologies in England and Wales, stakeholders and users provided conflicting reports. While stakeholders told McCartney that PG is used routinely, some stakeholders suggested that only STR testing is allowed by law enforcement in most investigations and that FDP and FIGG may be restricted; others reported that there were increasing instances of these technologies being utilized or piloted.

This "general confusion" around the use of forensic DNA technologies reinforces an ambiguous legal context, she said. Only two laws—the Police and Criminal Evidence Act (1984) and the Data Protection Act (2018)—have anything to say about the use of retained DNA profiles. McCartney explained that these laws have broad parameters and a lack of detail to guide potential users as to DNA use in law enforcement. For example, the Police and Criminal Evidence Act (1984) states that retained DNA must not be used other than "for purposes related to the prevention or detection of crime, the investigation of an offence or the conduct of a prosecution (or the identification of the deceased)" (c. 60). McCartney noted that if evidence from advanced forensic DNA technologies was to be used in court, the Criminal Procedure Rules and the Criminal Practice Directions would apply; she noted that these rules would be "highly problematic" for the admission of this DNA evidence.

A judicial primer on forensic DNA analysis is designed to inform courts for making decisions related to DNA evidence, but McCartney noted that its guidance is outdated and it does not include these technologies. The Forensic Information Database Board determines who can access the National DNA Database, said McCartney. They have yet to say anything about these new technologies being used but have previously agreed to the sending of samples overseas for such testing. Other entities—such as the Biometrics and Forensics Ethics group, the Forensic Regulator, the Biometrics Commissioner, and the Information Commissioner—look at individual aspects of forensic DNA technologies (e.g., privacy) but do not provide a wider or strategic, future-looking view.

When considering how to move forward, said McCartney, regulation of advanced forensic DNA technologies could take the form of law or code(s) of practice. Both options are complicated, she said. Laws are difficult to write well and would require determining what department would oversee advanced forensic DNA technologies, what the power and resources would be for oversight, and what legislative vehicle would be used. Relying on codes of practice can give the appearance of a practice being regulated when it is not, and determining what is "best practice" is rarely straightforward.

In conclusion, McCartney said oversight of advanced forensic DNA technologies in England and Wales is characterized by an overreliance on a disparate collection of policies, guidance, and codes of practice that are not publicly debated or publicly available. Current laws are confusing and overly broad, and there is no consensus on "best practice." Technological advances attract the attention of ethicists but there is far less attention paid to the regulation of these advances. She quoted the biometrics commissioner who said in 2018 that "actual deployment of new biometric technologies may lead to more legal challenges unless Parliament provides a clear, specific legal framework for the police use of new biometrics." Science is "marching on while law and regulation are still dragging their heels," said McCartney.

MULTIPLE LEVELS OF REGULATION IN SWITZERLAND

Martin Zieger, University of Bern, described the regulatory scheme in Switzerland around forensic DNA technologies. There are three levels of relevant regulation: the Criminal Procedure Code, the DNA Profiles Act (2003), and two technical ordinances. Together, these regulations determine whether and how advanced forensic DNA technologies can be used. Zieger reported that the DNA Profiles Act was recently revised to permit FDP (Revision of the DNA Profiles Act, 2023); this revision took 8 years from start to finish. Ziegler stated his understanding that FDP is currently restricted to serious offenses against physical and sexual integrity, and the use of FDP must be ordered by the public prosecutor, rather than the police. After 5 years of use of FDP, an evaluation will be conducted to see whether it has provided useful investigative leads, Zieger explained. He noted that the law specifically allows the ascertainment of eye, hair, and skin color; biogeographical origin; and age, and it specifically prohibits evaluating health-related or personal characteristics such as character, behavior, or intelligence. Zieger explained that when writing this law, parliament added a provision that allows the government to add permitted characteristics if "practical reliability is given." He said that while this was intended to allow the government to respond quickly to changes in technology without waiting for Parliament, it opens the door to an undemocratic process in which the executive power, based on recommendations from the federal police department, could make unilateral decisions. FDP has been permitted in Switzerland since August 2023, but Zieger said he knows of only one case that has used it.

FIGG is not regulated in Switzerland, so it is widely deemed inadmissible in court and is largely absent from the public debate. Zieger said that when the DNA Profiles Act was under revision (2023), only 2 out of 51 interested parties said that regulating FIGG was a priority. A national human genetic testing law has "harsh standards" for direct-to-consumer tests, which in theory makes it difficult for police to access consumer DNA databases. Switzerland law enforcement does engage in familial searching, but it is not widely used; he said that in the last 8 years there have been 20 cases in which familial searching was used, and only 1 in which it was successful.

PG is not mentioned in the DNA Profiles Act (2003), but all laboratory procedures are subject to control by the Swiss Accreditation Service. These standards require labs to participate in proficiency tests for any calculation software used in the lab. Zieger said that to his knowledge, two out of seven labs in Switzerland are using PG and one only uses it for operational casework. He hypothesized that the low uptake is because "most biologists are not big fans of statistics."

In closing, Zieger made three recommendations. First, he suggested that mass DNA tests should not be permitted based on FDP alone. Second, he called for rules for data access and the handling of incidental findings when conducting FDP or FIGG. Finally, he said that software validation and proper training are key for laboratories conducting PG.

GENERAL DATA PROTECTION REGULATION

A workshop audience member asked the panelists to comment on the General Data Protection Regulation (GDPR) and whether it impacts the use of forensic DNA technologies. McCartney replied that laws like the GDPR are often quite vague. There are provisions that say that the use of genetic data is prohibited, but a later provision provides a "massive get out clause" by allowing the use of genetic data if it is for law enforcement. Whether and how the law impacts the use of forensic DNA technologies depends on who is interpreting and overseeing the law, and whether guidance is provided about specific applications. Zieger added that GDPR explicitly excludes law enforcement use from the privacy law, but it does not give clear guidance on any limits of this exclusion. In his view, GDPR does not apply to the use of forensic DNA technologies for law enforcement. Instead, forensic DNA technologies are subject to the Law Enforcement Directive of the European Union, which leaves much leeway for implementation to the member states. Granja said that GDPR does impact FIGG because it explicitly requires users to give consent for their DNA to be used for law enforcement purposes.

BLIND TESTING

Following up on McNevin's mention of sequential unmasking of information, Norah Rudin, Forensic DNA Consulting, commented during the Q&A that she was part of an interdisciplinary group that introduced the process called sequential unmasking into the forensic space for use in casework. Blind testing, though standard in clinical testing, is generally not typical in forensic science, she said. As a compromise, her group came up with the idea of sequentially introducing information that could be relevant to the analysis of crime samples while staying as blind as possible for as long as possible. It ensures that labs receive the necessary data for a comprehensive and informed analysis while documenting how each piece of information is introduced and its impact on the conclusions drawn. Zieger added that, regarding proficiency testing, blind testing in the laboratory would mean receiving traces and not knowing that they are part of a test; he said this could be difficult to achieve but would be "really interesting" because it introduces some bias in the evaluation, if the analyst knows that they treat a test and not a real casework sample. Rudin replied that the method she and her colleagues developed for use in casework suggested using firewalls in the lab so that one person is communicating with law enforcement to obtain information about which samples are relevant to the questions in the case. The person doing the analytical work does not initially know, for example, the identity of the samples or what is the question in the case; these pieces of information are revealed as necessary going forward. Alicia Carriquiry, Iowa State University, added that while blind testing is challenging, it is not impossible. The Houston Forensic Science Center has been implementing blind testing in several disciplines for many years, she said, and there is an effort in Texas to implement blind testing across crime labs.

6

Moving Forward: Priorities for Research and Funding

The final session of the workshop featured a roundtable conversation about research gaps and funding needs for emerging forensic DNA technologies; the session was moderated by Michael Coble, University of North Texas Center for Human Identification. Coble asked panelists questions and invited workshop participants to share questions and comments.

HIGH-PRIORITY ACTIONABLE ISSUES

John Butler, National Institute of Standards and Technology, began the session by identifying several issues that had come up repeatedly at the workshop as key areas for further research and work; he noted that many of these were also identified in a Government Accountability Office (2021) report about forensic technology (see Box 6-1). These high-priority areas include

- increased training for law enforcement analysts and investigators to improve the consistent and objective use of forensic algorithms and understanding results;
- development and implementation of standards and policies;
- increased transparency related to the testing and performance of forensic algorithms to improve public trust;
- research on how to best communicate uncertainty in results; and
- independent verification and validation of software used in forensic DNA testing.

Disparate Impacts of Technology

Coble noted that the executive order that prompted this workshop emphasized the need to eliminate racial disparities in the criminal justice system and to strengthen bonds between law enforcement and communities. He asked panelists to comment on the potential disparate impact of emerging technologies, in particular the impact on communities that already experience fractured trust with law enforcement. Daphne Martschenko, Stanford University, responded that the community most impacted by an emerging technology often depends on the technology itself. For example, new treatments for rare genetic disorders primarily impact affluent White people. Other technologies, such as those used in law enforcement, tend to primarily impact communities that are historically underserved or exploited. One overarching pattern, however, is that the people who "shoulder the burden" of uncertain technologies are most often those who are already in vulnerable positions. Returning to the example of treatments for rare genetic disorders, the patients who take on the risks of uncertain new treatments are those who are in the vulnerable position of having a serious medical condition that has no approved treatment. Law enforcement technologies disproportionately impact Black and Brown communities that are vulnerable due to societal structures and racism. Given the different impacts of emerging technologies on different communities, said Martschenko, it is critical that assessments of risks and benefits include the voices of these communities.

Speakers at the workshop repeatedly described trade-offs between different risks and benefits—for example, independent verification of software versus the protection of trade secrets. These assessments are part of the implementation of any new technology, Martschenko said, and it is essential to consider who is defining the risks and benefits, what value they place on these risks and benefits, and how other stakeholders might view them differently. Matthews agreed and said that verification for law enforcement software usually involves weighing the risks to the developers against the risks to those "being decided about"—that is, the people involved or potentially involved in the criminal justice system. Matthews said that the criminal justice system should prioritize fairness to those being decided about. Our current system does not usually prioritize that population, she said; one reason is because errors in the system can be difficult to detect or acknowledge. If a plane crashes in part because of a software bug, there is an acknowledgment that an error has occurred. But if an individual is arrested and convicted in part because of a bug, the report of an error may be dismissed as simply the complaint of a guilty person. In this context, there is limited incentive for the iterative improvement of software, said Matthews.

Reliability

A priority area for research, said Coble, is ensuring the reliability of forensic DNA technologies. He asked panelists how reliability should be defined and how stakeholders could collaborate to support research on reliability. Butler said that *reliability* can be defined as trustworthiness, and it can be measured by the degree to which results are consistently accurate. Many people consider direct matching with a single-source DNA sample to be definitive and low risk, he said, but as technologies move out farther away from this traditional model, it becomes less clear what data the methods are based on and how reliable they are. Butler pointed to the National Academy of Sciences, National Academy of Engineering, and Institute of Medicine (2009) publication *On Being a Scientist: A Guide to Responsible Conduct in Research*, and said that a similar primer could be created for forensic DNA technologies.

Regarding facilitating collaboration between researchers, Martschenko said that this workshop has provided a valuable setting for cross-discipline conversations. Translating these conversations into action, however, is more difficult, and may require funding and academic incentives to encourage researchers to explore this area.

Funding as Leverage

Following on the topic of funding, Erin Murphy, New York University, said that federal funding has played an indispensable role in building the national network of databases and shaping what data are collected and what research is conducted. Funding can be a powerful lever for shifting focus through research funding and grants for casework, he said. Around $22 million was directed at clearing backlogs in 2022; these grants could have included conditions that reflected the best practices discussed at the workshop. For example, a grant for cold-case forensic investigative genetic genealogy work could include conditions that prohibit the generation of a single composite photo or that require the use of laboratories with accessible and transparent data.

Existing Frameworks

Coble asked panelists to identify fields, frameworks, or methodologies that could be useful in ensuring effective, ethical, and equitable use of these emerging technologies. Jeanna Matthews, Clarkson University, emphasized that software is increasingly being used in all disciplines, and requiring independent verification and validation is critical. She explained that the Institute of Electrical and Electronics Engineers' Standard 1012 is widely accepted throughout the U.S. government and should be used for any forensic software as well (see Box 3-4 in Chapter 3). Murphy said that with the use of these new technologies, forensic science should consider the ethical frameworks in fields such as health care.

Drawing from her professional experience, Martschenko explained that bioethicists have spent time considering the ethical and psychological impacts of revealing genetic information, and they could be useful in helping to determine where law enforcement should focus its efforts. Murphy explained that, in a related study that looked at 11,000 backlogged rape kits, researchers looked to other ethical frameworks to consider how reopening a decades-old case might impact the victim (Campbell et al., 2015). Martschenko then pointed to a program of the National Human Genome Research Institute called the ELSI Extramural Research Program. ELSI stands for ethical, legal, and social implications; the program is a mechanism for funding research on these implications in human genetics and genomics. This is one example, she said, of a framework outside the law enforcement arena that could be very useful in the ethical implementation of new technologies. Butler added that one way to bring other perspectives into the conversation is through exposure to other disciplines. For example, a forensic researcher might attend a molecular biology conference or a bioethics conference and then serve as an "ambassador" by bringing these perspectives back to their colleagues.

Federal Research Priorities

Coble asked the panel to imagine that they had the power to shape federal research priorities and asked them how they would use this power to design a request for proposal or to attach a condition to grant funding. Panelists had a number of suggestions:

- Require grant recipients to collect and report data from the research that was funded (e.g., how frequently does the use of forensic investigative genetic genealogy lead to a confirmed short tandem repeat match?). (Murphy)
- Fund a multistate survey that tracks violent crime and asks what tools were used to solve cases. (Murphy)
- Fund a multisite survey that compares crime rates and clearance rates in jurisdictions with different DNA policies. (Murphy)
- Fund qualitative and quantitative work on the impact of advanced forensic DNA technologies on Black and Native communities. (Murphy)

- Fund ELSI research on the impact of technologies, the risks and benefits to different groups, and strategies for minimizing harms and promoting benefits. (Martschenko)
- Fund independent verification and validation of software programs (Matthews) and require the resulting data to be publicly available. (Butler)
- Require public procurement funds to be spent on vendors that facilitate independent testing (e.g., agree to not use trade secret claims to impede electronic discovery obligations). (Matthews)
- Fund a grant to design and build training materials to help people understand the processes, limitations, and risks of new technologies. (Butler)
- Require research grantees to include a public education component around the research topic. (Murphy)
- When federal funding provides funding for the development of a tool, the tool should be open to scrutiny by the public and not protected by trade secret claims. (Coble)

Cross-Discipline Collaboration

Multiple discipline experts are involved in the development and deployment of forensic DNA technologies, said Murphy. It is important to respect their discipline expertise, acknowledge the boundaries of this expertise, and consider where and when additional expertise may be required. For example, she said, computer programmers working on autonomous vehicles could make decisions themselves about what lives to prioritize in what situation (e.g., the trolley problem, see Duignan, 2024), but the decision would likely be better informed if ethicists were involved. Martschenko agreed and told workshop participants about the Stanford University Institute for Human-Centered Artificial Intelligence, where ethicists partner with artificial intelligence researchers to work iteratively on identifying and mitigating potential societal harms.[1] There are also opportunities for experts in one area to be trained in other areas, she said. For example, graduate students in the genetics department at Stanford are seeking additional training and education on the ethical, social, and legal implications of genetic research. Field-specific training is important, she said, as is collaboration with colleagues who have expertise in other areas.

Murphy added that experts in law need to also be involved in these collaborations in order to identify and address potential legal consequences of genetic research. She gave the example of research seeking to identify a "violence gene" as a way to predict violent behavior. Defense attorneys, in their obligation to do everything in their power to prevent capital punish-

---

[1] See https://hai.stanford.edu/about

ment, have presented this research in court to show that their client was not entirely in control of his actions. The use of the gene in this way, said Murphy, opens the door to prosecutors arguing that people with the "violence gene" should be incarcerated to protect public safety. Conversations about these complicated issues need to be informed by experts across multiple disciplines, said Murphy, and a cross-disciplinary approach is critical for making rules about the use of new technologies.

Ray Wickenheiser, New York State Police Crime Lab System, said that vendors should be included in these conversations because understanding the concerns, needs, and requirements of different stakeholders will inform their redesign and improvement process. Murphy responded that there is little incentive for a highly lucrative vendor market to be engaged in these conversations, and that vendors are more likely to be engaged in improvement efforts if there are concrete consequences for providing software that is not validated or for operating without transparency. Consequences are more powerful for changing behavior than hearing critiques, she said.

Regulation and Oversight

Due to a lack of regulation and governance around forensic DNA technologies, said a workshop audience member, "regulation of a lot of these technologies really only happens in a criminal trial." However, he said, relying on this type of "regulation" is problematic for two reasons. First, he pointed to existing bias toward prosecutors in admissibility hearings; a study of *Daubert* hearings in Wisconsin found that the prosecution was successful in 114 out of 114 cases. Second, he noted that if advanced forensic DNA technologies are used only for investigatory purposes, the prosecution does not have an obligation to turn over the information as exculpatory evidence. Murphy acknowledged these as serious concerns, noting that the most direct lever to address the issue is the federal government. She explained that the federal government is a huge source of funding and serves as a policy model for states. Murphy said that she hopes that a federal policy would follow a similar approach to Maryland Criminal Procedure Code Section 17-102 (see Box 2-4 in Chapter 2), with strong declarations of standards for use. In addition, if federal grants or assistance are given to conduct forensic DNA testing, funding could be conditioned on disclosure during trial. However, she said, most criminal cases—greater than 90%—do not end up in court because the defendant pleads out. While the assumption is that forensic DNA technologies will be regulated by the criminal system, "it is very much not going to be regulated by the system." A few lawyers on high-profile cases may challenge the use of advanced forensic DNA technologies, but these challenges become difficult after the technologies have been in use in the justice system for several years. In the absence of real regulation, Murphy encouraged a strategy of conditioning research and casework funding on mandates for disclosure and transparency.

Throughout the workshop, individual speakers identified resources for those interested in learning more about forensic DNA technologies. These are listed in Box 6-1.

BOX 6-1
Further Reading

- Genetic Science Learning Center: https://learn.genetics.utah.edu
- Personal Genetics Education and Dialogue: https://pged.org
- *Forensic Technology: Algorithms Strengthen Forensic Analysis, but Several Factors Can Affect Outcomes* (Government Accountability Office, 2021): https://www.gao.gov/assets/gao-21-435sp.pdf
- *On Being a Scientist: A Guide to Responsible Conduct in Research: Third Edition* (National Academies of Sciences, Engineering, and Medicine [National Academies], 2009): https://nap.nationalacademies.org/catalog/12192/on-being-a-scientist-a-guide-to-responsible-conduct-in
- *Long-Term Vision and Strategic Priorities for Forensic Science in the United States: Summary Report of a Roundtable Discussion with Thought Leaders* (Swofford, 2024): https://www.nist.gov/publications/long-term-vision-and-strategic-priorities-forensic-science-united-states-summary-report
- *Forensic DNA Analysis: A Primer for Courts* (The Royal Society): https://royalsociety.org/~/media/about-us/programmes/science-and-law/royal-society-forensic-dna-analysis-primer-for-courts.pdf
- *Making Sense of Forensic Genetics* (Sense about Science, 2017) https://senseaboutscience.org/activities/making-sense-of-forensic-genetics
- *Understanding Forensic DNA* (Suzanne Bell & John M. Butler, 2022) https://www.cambridge.org/core/books/understanding-forensicdna/B585963556536C8FF47CD0F8FE6401D9
- *National Technology Validation and Implementation Collaborative (NTVIC) policies and procedures for Forensic Investigative Genetic Genealogy (FIGG)* (Wickenheiser et al., 2023): https://www.sciencedirect.com/science/article/pii/S2589871X23000037?via%3Dihub
- *Interim Policy on Forensic Genetic Genealogical DNA Analysis and Searching* (U.S. Department of Justice, 2019) https://www.justice.gov/olp/page/file/1204386/dl
- *Strengthening Forensic Science in the United States: A Path Forward* (National Academies, 2009): https://nap.nationalacademies.org/catalog/12589/strengthening-forensic-science-in-the-united-states-a-path-forward

SOURCE: Generated by the rapporteur based on comments from speakers on March 13 and 14, 2024.

CLOSING REFLECTIONS

At the close of the workshop, planning committee members and other workshop participants and audience members offered their thoughts on key themes and remaining issues.

Education and Training

One of the key points conveyed at the workshop, said Heather McKiernan, RTI International, was the importance of education and training of all players in the system, from investigators to medical examiners to attorneys. However, "education alone will not solve all of our problems"; regulation and oversight are necessary. Coble also highlighted the importance of education and training for all stakeholders affected by advanced forensic DNA technologies, noting that this will require an investment of resources. Alicia Carriquiry, Iowa State University, said that judges and attorneys are a priority for education. Most legal professionals are ill equipped to understand and convey the details of advanced forensic DNA technologies, she said, let alone conduct a robust cross-examination to interrogate their reliability and limitations.

Matthews explained that in her experience, it is a rare judge who is willing to take the time to understand the science enough to make an informed decision about admissibility. She said that when judges are willing to really look at the science, she has seen the prosecution pull scientific evidence so that the judge cannot make a ruling on it. Asking judges or defense attorneys to be the stopgap against potentially unreliable technologies is "not a great use of our societal resources," she said. Norah Rudin, Forensic DNA Consulting, echoed Matthews's observation that sometimes evidence is pulled, or a case is settled rather that going to trial, to avoid shedding light on problematic issues. She said that she and her colleagues made an effort a few years ago to educate judges, and they were unsuccessful. A major reason for their lack of success, she said, is that judges tend to only want to be educated by other judges. This is a major roadblock that needs to be addressed.

Culture of Science

Forensic tools "arise from a culture of law enforcement and not a culture of science," said Natalie Ram, University of Maryland King Carey School of Law. This was stated in the landmark National Research Council (2009) report *Strengthening Forensic Science in the United States: A Path Forward*, and remains a persistent pattern today with these new technologies. We need to strengthen the culture of science in the forensic space by encouraging adoption of scientific values such as transparency, standardization, validation, and independence, she said. Wickenheiser said that as a forensic scientist, he considers his duty to science. He explained that this means bringing the best technology to criminal cases, aiming to get it right, acknowledging when things go wrong, and taking steps to continuously improve.

Craig O'Connor, New York City Office of Chief Medical Examiner, said that scientists, laboratories, and other stakeholders are aware of the concerns that have been presented at this workshop, and that they are changing processes to address some of the concerns. For example, labs continue to evaluate new standards, guidelines, and recommendations; forensic science commissions have been put in place; labs are undergoing accreditation; and some states have published road maps on best practices for DNA technologies. Lab scientists are accustomed to being transparent, said O'Connor; they document each step in lab notebooks and publish data in peer-reviewed journals. O'Connor encouraged defense attorneys and their experts to reach out to labs to talk about the technologies used and the results obtained. "The last thing we want to hear is that some plea deal was taken with no communication done with the laboratory itself," he said, emphasizing the need for communication and education between laboratories, courts, and members of the legal community.

Regulation and Oversight

McKiernan said that there is a need for policies, guidance, and codes of practice with federal or state oversight; self-regulation is insufficient. There is a need for research on the tools themselves as well as the societal impacts of the tools, and this research needs to be done in collaboration with other stakeholders to understand the downstream implications. Sarah Chu, Perlmutter Center for Legal Justice at Cardozo Law, agreed that guidance has limited utility; governance and regulation are necessary. Regulations often tackle one technology at a time, but "legislation will always lag tech development" if we do not use governance to address classes of technology, she said. This governance system must be the result of a collaboration among multiple stakeholders, including the impacted communities, and not at the "whim of law enforcement agencies." We need to be mindful of "noble cause corruption and thin ethics," otherwise appeals to public safety can shut down conversations about who benefits, who is harmed, and what justice means in the application of technology, stated Chu.

Carriquiry offered a summary of best practices for effective regulation and oversight of probabilistic genotyping (PG), based on the discussions among panelists from the PG session. First, PG systems should be subject to peer review by independent researchers who have no stake in the outcome.

Second, vendors of PG systems should not be allowed to use contract law to block independent review. Third, trade secret claims should not be allowed to impede electronic discovery obligations to disclose relevant evidence in criminal cases. Implementation of these best practices, she said, could be achieved through procurement guidelines and grant requirements.

Formal Systems of Repair

Chu called for the establishment of formal systems of repair when mistakes are made or errors occur. She suggested that this system should include the duty to correct and notify, conducting root and cultural cause analyses to reduce risk of reoccurrence, and establishing committees of diverse constituents to notify impacted people in a publicly accountable process. Creating these systems is the responsibility of the government as the sponsor of criminal cases, said Chu. O'Connor agreed that formal systems of repair are critical and added that this system should bring mistakes to light in a constructive rather than punitive manner. Dealing with mistakes through an open process will prevent laboratories from hiding mistakes for fear of punishment and will allow problematic aspects of the technologies to be addressed while strengthening the reliability of other aspects. O'Connor said that "we shouldn't let anecdotal success stories […] drive the use of these technologies if they are unreliable." At the same time, he said, "we shouldn't let anecdotal bad actors lead us to throw the baby out with the bathwater" and not use technologies that have been proven reliable.

Chu said that cultural frameworks in aviation and health care are relevant here; these frameworks protect or incentivize people to come forward with problems they are aware of. Implementing this type of framework will require collaboration among multiple entities in the system to create a culture of accountability without fear of punishment. Martschenko drew an analogy between this proposed framework and how clinical trials deal with adverse events. In clinical trial research, there are clear criteria for what constitutes an adverse event, and the trial might be paused if a participant experiences a serious adverse event. In the context of forensic DNA technologies, she continued, there could be clear criteria established for what type of error or unexpected result requires reporting, and use of the tool might pause while the error is investigated.

Next Steps

Given the challenges and roadblocks discussed at the workshop, Chu identified several areas in which action could be taken. The federal government needs to support the development of a framework for oversight of advanced forensic DNA technologies, she said. In addition to validation of tools prior to implementation, the framework should regulate how data are collected, used, retained, and expunged. Frameworks in the areas of artificial intelligence, genomics, and predictive policing could serve as models for this new framework. In the absence of a federal entity to regulate investigative and forensic methods and technologies, Chu said there is a need for interagency processes to bring more perspectives to the table. For example, the U.S. Department of Justice could convene diverse constituents of the forensic evidence ecosystem, including impacted communities, and make these convenings accessible and meaningful to stakeholders. This could require going out into communities and speaking through credible messengers to communicate with hard-to-reach communities, she said. Federal funding—through procurement, research funding, and grants—can be used as a lever to encourage more ethical implementation of advanced forensic DNA technologies. Chu pointed to the Federal Bureau of Investigation's quality assurance framework and accreditation requirements for access to the Combined DNA Index System, and she suggested that a similar approach could be used for access to genetic databases.

In short, said Chu, the field of forensic DNA technologies needs validity, reliability, and accountability. Implementing such a system will require research, collaboration, transparency, and collective conversations, and all of these require resources. Throughout this work, she said, "we need to infuse every step of discussions with values and what we owe to each other in the context of the American criminal legal system, where we know that overpoliced and vulnerable communities will bear a concentrated harm from misuse of methods and technologies that may not be visible to nonmarginalized communities."

Butler closed by quoting Marie Curie, who said, "I was taught that the way of progress was neither swift nor easy." This workshop identified a number of priority areas in which action needs to be taken, he said, and this will require a commitment to keep moving forward. The work will not be "swift or easy"; any project of importance takes time and effort.

References

Academy Standards Board. (2021). *Formulating propositions for likelihood ratios in forensic DNA interpretations*. https://www.aafs.org/sites/default/files/media/documents/041_Std_Ballot02.pdf

Australian Federal Police. (2023). *Privacy impact assessment: Pilot of forensic/investigative genetic genealogy*. https://www.afp.gov.au/sites/default/files/2023-09/LEX%201843%20Document.pdf

Australian Law Reform Commission. (2010). *DNA database systems*. https://www.alrc.gov.au/publication/essentially-yours-the-protection-of-human-genetic-information-in-australia-alrc-report-96/43-dna-database-systems/dna-database-systems/

Bell, S., & Butler, J. M. (2022). *Understanding forensic DNA*. Cambridge University Press. https://doi.org/10.1017/9781009043311

Butler, J. M. (2006). Genetics and genomics of core short tandem repeat loci used in human identity testing. *Journal of Forensic Sciences*, *51*(2), 253–265.

Campbell, R., Shaw, J., & Fehler-Cabral, G. (2015). Shelving justice: The discovery of thousands of untested rape kits in Detroit. *City & Community*. https://doi.org/10.1111/cico.12108

Carter, M. (2024, March 4). WA man released as cold-case murder suspect sues detective. *Seattle Times*. https://www.seattletimes.com/seattle-news/law-justice/wa-man-released-as-cold-case-murder-suspect-sues-detective/

Data Protection Act, c. 12. (2018). U.K. Public General Acts. https://www.legislation.gov.uk/ukpga/2018/12/contents/enacted

Daubert v. Merrell Dow Pharmaceuticals, Inc., 509 U.S. 579 (1993). https://supreme.justia.com/cases/federal/us/509/579

Duignan, B. (2024). Trolley problem. *Britannica*. https://www.britannica.com/topic/trolley-problem

Exec. Order No. 14,074, 3 C.F.R. 32945 (2022). https://www.federalregister.gov/documents/2022/05/31/2022-11810/advancing-effective-accountable-policing-and-criminal-justice-practices-to-enhance-public-trust-and

Federal Act on the Use of DNA Profiles in Criminal Proceedings and for Identifying Unidentified or Missing Persons (DNA Profies Act). (2023). Swiss Confederation. https://www.fedlex.admin.ch/eli/cc/2004/811/en

Federal Bureau of Investigation. (n.d.-a). *CODIS and NDIS fact sheet*. https://www.fbi.gov/how-we-can-help-you/dna-fingerprint-act-of-2005-expungement-policy/codis-and-ndis-fact-sheet

———. (n.d.-b). *Law enforcement resources: Combined DNA Index System (CODIS)*. https://le.fbi.gov/science-and-lab/biometrics-and-fingerprints/codis

Gill, P., Gusmão, L., Haned, H., Mayr, W. R., Morling, N., Parson, W., Prieto, L., Prinz, M., Schneider, H., Schneider, P. M., & Weir, B. S. (2012). DNA commission of the International Society of Forensic Genetics: Recommendations on the evaluation of STR typing results that may include drop-out and/or drop-in using probabilistic methods. *Forensic Science International: Genetics*, 6(6), 679–688. https://doi.org/10.1016/j.fsigen.2012.06.002

Government Accountability Office. (2021). *Forensic technology: Algorithms strengthen forensic analysis, but several factors can affect outcomes*. https://www.gao.gov/products/gao-19-216

Guerrini, C. J., Robinson, J. O., Petersen, D., & McGuire, A. L. (2018). Should police have access to genetic genealogy databases? Capturing the Golden State Killer and other criminals using a controversial new forensic technique. *PLoS Biology*, 16(10), e2006906. https://doi.org/10.1371/journal.pbio.2006906

Hunter, L. (2019, March 17). Right on. Genetics is a poor solution to violence [Post]. X. https://twitter.com/ProfLHunter/status/1107340012213800960

Institute of Electrical and Electronics Engineers (IEEE). (2017). IEEE Standard for System, Software, and Hardware Verification and Validation (1012-2016). https://ieeexplore.ieee.org/document/8055462

Investigative Genetic Genealogy Accreditation Board. (2024). *Standards*. https://www.iggab.org/standards.html

Justice in Forensic Algorithms Act, H. R. 7394, 118th Cong. (2024). https://www.congress.gov/bill/118th-congress/house-bill/7394/text

Maryland Criminal Procedure Code § 17-102 (2024). https://mgaleg.maryland.gov/mgawebsite/Laws/StatuteText?article=gcp&section=17-102&enactments=false

Maryland Governor's Office of Crime Prevention and Policy. (n.d.). *Reports and publications, criminal justice reports*. https://goccp.maryland.gov/reports-and-publications/

McNevin, D., Wright, K., Barash, M., Gomes, S., Jamieson, A., & Chaseling, J. (2021). Proposed framework for comparison of continuous probabilistic genotyping systems amongst different laboratories. *Forensic Sciences*, 1(1), 33–45. https://doi.org/10.3390/forensicsci1010006

Monterio v. Cormier, 1:21-cv-00046 (1st Cir., 2023). https://casetext.com/case/monteiro-v-cormier-1

National Academies of Sciences, Engineering, and Medicine (National Academies). (2015). Support for *Forensic science research: Improving the scientific role of the National Institute of Justice*. The National Academies Press. https://doi.org/10.17226/21772

———. (2023). *Reducing racial inequality in crime and justice: Science, practice, and policy*. National Academies Press. https://doi.org/10.17226/26705

National Academy of Sciences, National Academy of Engineering, and Institute of Medicine. (2009). *On being a scientist: A guide to responsible conduct in research*. National Academies Press. https://doi.org/10.17226/12192

National Human Genome Research Institute. (2024). *Allele*. https://www.genome.gov/genetics-glossary/Allele

National Institute of Justice. (2011). *What is STR analysis?* https://nij.ojp.gov/topics/articles/what-str-analysis

National Research Council. (2009). *Strengthening forensic science in the United States: A path forward*. National Academies Press. http://www.nap.edu/catalog/12589.html

New South Wales (NSW) Police Force. (n.d.). *Forensic investigative genetic genealogy*. https://www.police.nsw.gov.au/about_us/information_of_interest_to_the_community/forensic_investigative_genetic_genealogy

Office of the Australian Information Commissioner. (2021). *Guide to undertaking privacy impact assessments*. https://www.oaic.gov.au/privacy/privacy-guidance-for-organisations-and-government-agencies/privacy-impact-assessments/guide-to-undertaking-privacy-impact-assessments

Organization of Scientific Area Committees for Forensic Science. (2018). *Assigning propositions for likelihood ratios*. https://www.nist.gov/system/files/documents/2020/05/08/assigning_propositions_for_likelihood_ratios_OSAC%20PROPOSED.pdf

Police and Criminal Evidence Act § 60. (1984). U.K. Public General Acts. https://www.legislation.gov.uk/ukpga/1984/60/section/63

Revision of the DNA Profiles Act. (2023, May 15). Swiss Federal Office of Police. https://www.fedpol.admin.ch/fedpol/en/home/sicherheit/personenidentifikation-neu/dna-und-codis/dna-profilgesetz.html

Scientific Working Group on DNA Analysis Methods (SWGDAM). (2023). *Guidelines for the validation of probabilistic genotyping systems*. https://www.swgdam.org/_files/ugd/4344b0_22776006b67c4a32a5ffc04fe3b56515.pdf

Sense about Science. (2020). *Making sense of forensic genetics*. https://senseaboutscience.org/activities/making-sense-of-forensic-genetics/

Shestak, A. G., Bukaeva, A. A., Saber, S., & Zaklyazminskaya, E. V. (2021). Allelic dropout is a common phenomenon that reduces the diagnostic yield of PCR-based sequencing of targeted gene panels. *Frontiers in Genetics*, *12*, 620337. https://doi.org/10.3389/fgene.2021.620337

Sogorea Te' Land Trust. (2021). *Rematriation resource guide*. https://sogoreate-landtrust.org/wp-content/uploads/2021/07/Rematriation-Resource-Guide.pdf

Swofford, H. (2024). *Long-term vision and strategic priorities for forensic science in the United States: Summary Report of a roundtable discussion with thought leaders, special publication (NIST SP)*. National Institute of Standards and Technology. https://doi.org/10.6028/NIST.SP.2100-06

Tsosie, K. S., Yracheta, J. M., Kolopenuk, J. A., & Geary, J. (2021). We have "gifted" enough: Indigenous genomic data sovereignty in precision medicine. *American Journal of Bioethics*, *21*(4), 72–75. https://doi.org/10.1080/15265161.2021.1891347

U.K. Home Office. (2018). *Biometrics strategy: Better public services maintaining public trust*. https://assets.publishing.service.gov.uk/media/5b34f69c40f0b60b107a4a80/Home_Office_Biometrics_Strategy_-_2018-06-28.pdf

U.S. Department of Justice (DOJ). (2019, November 1). *Interim policy: Forensic genetic genealogical DNA analysis and searching*. https://www.justice.gov/olp/page/file/1204386/dl

Utah Public Safety Code § 53-10-403.7 (2023). Investigative genetic genealogy service. https://le.utah.gov/xcode/Title53/Chapter10/53-10-S403.7.html?v=C53-10-S403.7_2023050320230503

Wakelin, J., & Mendes, J. (2023). *DNA discovery*. ABC News, October 7. https://www.abc.net.au/news/2023-10-08/how-genetic-genealogy-is-solving-australias-coldest-cases/102870058

Weir, B. S., & Zheng, X. (2015). SNPs and SNVs in forensic science. *Forensic Science International. Genetics Supplement Series*, *5*, e267–e268. https://doi.org/10.1016/j.fsigss.2015.09.106

Wickenheiser, R. A., Naugle, J., Hoey, B., Nowlin, R., Kumar, S. A., Kubinski, M. A., Glynn, C., Valerio, R., Allen, L., Stoiloff, S., Kochanski, J., Guerrini, C., & Schubert, A. M. (2023). National Technology Validation and Implementation Collaborative (NTVIC): Guidelines for establishing Forensic Investigative Genetic Genealogy (FIGG) programs. *Forensic Science International: Synergy*, 7, 100446. https://doi.org/10.1016/j.fsisyn.2023.100446

Worth, K. (2018). *Framed for murder by his own DNA*. The Marshall Project. https://www.themarshallproject.org/2018/04/19/framed-for-murder-by-his-own-dna

Appendix A

Public Meeting Agendas

COMMITTEE ON LAW AND JUSTICE AND COMPUTER SCIENCE AND TELECOMMUNICATIONS BOARD

The National Academy of Sciences Building,
2101 Constitution Ave., NW
Washington, DC 20002

**MARCH 13–14, 2024
ROOM 120**

Guiding Questions:

- How are probabilistic genotyping, facial predictions, and genetic genealogy being used by law enforcement across federal, state, local, tribal, and territorial agencies?
- How reliable and accurate are these methods in practice?
- What are the relevant legal considerations and precedents that accompany these new technologies?
- What are the disparate impact concerns raised by these technologies or their manner of use?
- What considerations (e.g., accuracy of these technologies, including underlying issues of sensitivity and specificity; privacy, civil rights, civil liberties; and disparate impact) need to be assessed in implementing these technologies and the use of genetic material by law enforcement?

- What are institutional considerations for operations and procedures to ensure that these technologies are being used effectively and equitably?

WEDNESDAY, MARCH 13, 2024

9:00–9:15   Welcome and Introduction
Alicia Carriquiry, *Iowa State University; Chair, Workshop Planning Committee*
Lucas Zarwell, *National Institute of Justice*
Craig O'Connor, *New York City Office of Chief Medical Examiner; Workshop Planning Committee Member*
Heather McKiernan, *RTI International; Workshop Planning Committee Member*

9:15–10:30   Setting the Stage: Considering Ethics, Equity, and Accountability
Tierra Bradford, *The Leadership Conference on Civil and Human Rights*
Jennifer Lynch, *Electronic Frontier Foundation*
Daphne Martschenko, *Stanford University*
Krystal Tsosie, *Arizona State University*
Moderator: Sarah Chu, *Perlmutter Center for Legal Justice at Cardozo Law; Workshop Planning Committee Member*

10:30–10:45   BREAK

10:45–12:00   Surveying the Landscape: DNA Technology Use in the Criminal Legal System [Virtual]
Paul Belli, *International Homicide Investigators Association*
Leigh Clark, *Florida Department of Law Enforcement*
Daniel Katz, *Maryland Department of State Police, Forensic Sciences Division*
Mark Pooley, *The Center for Human Identification, University of North Texas*
Jeremy Triplett, *Kentucky State Police Central Forensic Laboratory*
Raymond Valerio, *Queen's County District Attorney's Office*
Moderator: Craig O'Connor, *New York City Office of Chief Medical Examiner; Workshop Planning Committee Member*

APPENDIX A 95

12:00–1:00		LUNCH
1:00–2:15		Forensic Investigative Genetic Genealogy (FIGG): Considerations for Implementation
Ray Wickenheiser, *New York State Police Crime Lab System*
Claire Glynn, *University of New Haven*
Erin Murphy, *New York University*
Christi Guerrini, *Baylor College of Medicine* (virtual)
Discussant: Krystal Tsosie, *Arizona State University*
Moderator: Heather McKiernan, *RTI International; Workshop Planning Committee Member*
2:15–2:30		BREAK
2:30–4:00		Probabilistic Genotyping Software (PG): Considerations for Implementation
Todd Bille, *National Laboratory Center, U.S. Bureau of Alcohol, Tobacco, Firearms and Explosives*
Jeanna Matthews, *Clarkson University*
Norah Rudin, *Forensic DNA Consulting*
Rebecca Wexler, *University of California, Berkeley* (virtual)
Discussant: Sarah Chu, *Perlmutter Center for Legal Justice at Cardozo Law; Workshop Planning Committee Member*
Moderator: Alicia Carriquiry, *Iowa State University; Chair, Workshop Planning Committee*
4:00		MEETING ADJOURNS—END OF DAY 1

THURSDAY, MARCH 14, 2024

9:00–9:30	Welcome and Reflections from Day 1
Alicia Carriquiry, *Iowa State University; Chair, Workshop Planning Committee* with Workshop Planning Committee members
9:30–10:45	Forensic DNA Phenotyping (FDP): Considerations for Implementation
Susan Walsh, *Indiana University Indianapolis*
Rebecca Brown, *Maat Strategies*
Matthias Wienroth, *Northumbria University* (virtual)

Discussant: Daphne Martschenko, *Stanford University*
Moderator: Alicia Carriquiry, *Iowa State University; Chair, Workshop Planning Committee*

10:45–11:00   **BREAK**

11:00–12:00   **Learning from Abroad: Law Enforcement Use of DNA Technology Outside of the United States [Virtual]**
Dennis McNevin, *University of Technology Sydney* (virtual)
Rafaela Granja, *Communication and Society Research Centre, University of Minho, Portugal* (virtual)
Carole McCartney, *University of Leicester Law School* (virtual)
Martin Zieger, *University of Bern* (virtual)
Moderator: Natalie Ram, *University of Maryland King Carey School of Law; Workshop Planning Committee Member*

12:00–1:00   **LUNCH**

1:00–2:00   **Future Research Needs**
John Butler, *National Institute of Standards and Technology*
Daphne Martschenko, *Stanford University*
Jeanna Matthews, *Clarkson University*
Erin Murphy, *New York University*
Moderator: Michael Coble, *University of North Texas Center for Human Identification; Workshop Planning Committee Member*

2:00–3:00   **Closing Reflections**
Alicia Carriquiry, *Iowa State University; Chair, Workshop Planning Committee* with Workshop Planning Committee members

3:00   **MEETING ADJOURNS—END OF DAY 2**

Appendix B

Workshop Planning Committee and Speaker Biographies

WORKSHOP PLANNING COMMITTEE

ALICIA CARRIQUIRY (*Chair*, she/her/hers) is professor of statistics at Iowa State University. She previously was associate provost at Iowa State. Carriquiry's research interests are in Bayesian statistics and general methods. Her recent work focuses on nutrition and dietary assessment, as well as on problems in genomics, forensic sciences, and traffic safety. Carriquiry is an elected member of the International Statistical Institute and a fellow of the American Statistical Association. She serves on the Executive Committee of the Institute of Mathematical Statistics and is a member of the Board of Trustees of the National Institute of Statistical Sciences. She is also a past president of the International Society for Bayesian Analysis and a past member of the Board of the Plant Sciences Institute at Iowa State University. Carriquiry is editor of *Statistical Sciences and of Bayesian Analysis*, and serves on the editorial boards of several Latin American journals of statistics and mathematics. She is a member of the Federal Steering Committee Future Directions for the CSFII/NHANES Diet/Nutrition Survey: What We Eat in America. Carriquiry received a M.Sc. in animal science from the University of Illinois, and a M.Sc. in statistics and a Ph.D. in statistics and animal genetics from Iowa State University. She has served on three National Academy of Sciences committees: the Subcommittee on Interpretation and Uses of Dietary Reference Intakes; the Committee on Evaluation of USDA's Methodology for Estimating Eligibility and Participation for the WIC Program; and the Committee on Third Party Toxicity Research with Human Research Participants. Currently, she is a member of the standing

Committee on Applied and Theoretical Statistics of the National Research Council, the Committee on Assessing the Feasibility, Accuracy and Technical Capability of a Ballistics National Database of the National Research Council and of the Committee on Gender Differences in the Careers in Science, Mathematics and Engineering Faculty of the National Academy of Sciences.

SARAH CHU (she/her/hers) is the director of policy and reform and leads the Perlmutter Center's forensic science policy initiatives. Prior to joining the Perlmutter Center, she led the Innocence Project's policy portfolio on forensic science, forensic medicine, and police investigative technologies for 15 years. Chu's research interests include oversight and accountability of criminal investigative and forensic science methods and technologies; their ethical, legal, and social implications; and capacity for just and equitable implementation. She served on the Scientific Inquiry and Research Subcommittee of the National Commission on Forensic Science and was the 2021 recipient of the Legal Aid Society's Magnus Mukoro Award for Integrity in Forensic Science. Chu is also member of the Harvard Medical School Center for Bioethics Fellowship Program. She holds both a B.S. in biochemistry/cell biology and communication as well as an M.S. in biology from University of California, San Diego, an M.S. in epidemiology from Stanford University, and completed her doctorate in criminal justice at John Jay College of Criminal Justice/CUNY Graduate Center.

MICHAEL COBLE (he/him/his) is an associate professor and the executive director of the Center for Human Identification at the University of North Texas Health Science Center in Fort Worth, Texas. He was a National Research Center post-doctoral fellow at the National Institute of Standards and Technology. Coble has more than 100 peer-reviewed publications in the areas of forensic DNA analysis and interpretation and is recognized among the top 2% of highly cited researcher worldwide, and in the top 100 of highly cited researchers in the United States in the area of forensic and legal medicine. He is a fellow of the American Academy of Forensic Sciences. Over his 28-year career in forensics, Coble has helped to resolve a number of high-profile historical cases using DNA testing, including the two missing Romanov children and the unknown child of the RSS Titanic. He first characterized a set of novel non-CODIS DNA markers useful for degraded DNA, three of which have been adopted world-wide as standard markers for current DNA testing. Coble received his B.S. in biology from the Appalachian State University, his M.S. in forensic science (concentration in molecular biology), and his Ph.D. in genetics from The George Washington University.

HEATHER McKIERNAN (she/her/hers) is currently the senior manager of forensics at RTI International, where she serves as the forensic services program manager for the National Missing and Unidentified Persons System. In this capacity, she facilitates forensic and analytical services including anthropology, odontology, fingerprint analysis, traditional DNA testing, and forensic genetic genealogy for missing, unidentified, and unclaimed persons cases across the United States. McKiernan is an accomplished professional with experience spanning academia, research, casework, and executive leadership as a laboratory director overseeing operations. Throughout her career, she has worked to develop best practices for forensic evidence collection, testing, interpretation, and presentation in court. McKiernan is a fellow of the American Academy of Forensic Sciences, the International Society of Forensic Genetics (ISFG), and a member of the Vidocq cold case investigation unit. She has served as a guest editor for the *Journal Forensic Science International: Genetics*, co-chair of the 2022 ISFG Congress, as a member of the Organization of Scientific Area Committees for Forensic Science's Biological Data and Reporting Subcommittee, and past president of the Council of Forensic Science Educators. McKiernan received her M.S. in forensic science from Arcadia University and her Ph.D. in biological sciences from the University of Denver.

CRAIG O'CONNOR (he/him/his) is currently deputy director in the Forensic Biology Department of the New York City Office of Chief Medical Examiner, the largest public forensic DNA laboratory in the United States with a staff of more than 200. He oversees laboratory functions involving the processing of evidentiary material from a range of case types using DNA methods, applying statistical analysis using probabilistic genotyping to those cases as well as bringing on new and emerging technologies. O'Connor also holds a position as clinical assistant professor in the Department of Forensic Medicine at New York University Grossman School of Medicine and previous adjunct positions at John Jay College of Criminal Justice and the College of Mount St. Vincent's having taught courses in forensic biology and forensic science. He has provided expert testimonies more than 80 times in jurisdictions inside and outside of New York City at the local and federal level, including admissibility hearings about the general acceptance of DNA technologies. O'Connor is a fellow in the American Academy of Forensic Sciences as well as a member of the International Society of Forensic Genetics and the American Society of Crime Laboratory Directors and a trained Technical Assessor of the ANSI National Accreditation Board. He received an M.S. and Ph.D. in genetics and genomics from the University of Connecticut with an emphasis in forensic DNA identification and population genetics.

NATALIE RAM (she/her/hers) is professor of law at the University of Maryland Francis King Carey School of Law and adjunct faculty with the Berman Institute of Bioethics at Johns Hopkins University. She is a leading scholar on the intersection of genetic privacy and the criminal legal system, including investigative genetic genealogy and the development and trade secrecy surrounding privately developed probabilistic genotyping tools. Ram is an elected member of the American Law Institute, and she was a Greenwall Faculty Scholar in Bioethics. She previously clerked for Associate Justice Stephen G. Breyer, U.S. Supreme Court, and for Judge Guido Calabresi, U.S. Court of Appeals for the Second Circuit. Ram earned her J.D. at Yale Law School and A.B. in public and international affairs at Princeton University.

WORKSHOP SPEAKERS

TODD BILLE (he/him/his) began his forensic career at the Indiana State Police Laboratory in Indianapolis and performed the first DNA analysis on casework for the ISP Laboratory. He later was selected to be the DNA Technical Leader and a supervisor. He later moved to The Bode Technology Group as the assistant laboratory director and later the vice president of special projects. While at The Bode Technology Group, Bille led the research efforts investigating improved DNA extraction methods from skeletal remains used for the victims of the September 11 attacks and other mass fatality events. He also performed research on various topics related to "touch DNA." Following this, Bille was hired by the Bureau of Alcohol, Tobacco, Firearms and Explosives Laboratory as the DNA Technical Leader to start the DNA Unit. Since then, the research performed at the ATF Laboratory has focused on improving the DNA analysis of "touch DNA" samples from incendiary devices, firearms/fired cartridge cases, and explosive devices. Bille is certified through the American Board of Criminalistics and a member of the American Academy of Forensic Sciences and the International Society for Forensic Genetics. He received his B.S. degree in biochemistry from Purdue University and his M.S. degree from Indiana University Purdue University at Indianapolis.

PAUL BELLI (he/him/his) retired from the Sacramento County Sheriff's Office after 24 years serving in his last assignment as the Centralized Investigations Division assistant commander. In his tenure with the sheriff's office, he served assignments as a lieutenant, patrol officer, field training officer, motor officer, firearms instructor, force options instructor, and Evoc instructor. Upon selection to detectives, Belli was assigned to the Sexual Assault and Elder Abuse Bureau before being selected to join the Homicide Bureau where he spent 7 years as a homicide detective. Upon promotion to sergeant, he was again assigned to homicide as the bureau supervisor. As a manager Belli served as a patrol watch commander, assistant commander of the Main Jail Division, and assistant commander for the Centralized Investigations Division. He is a State of California's Commission on Peace Officer Standards and Training instructor for the Officer Involved Shooting investigations course, a past committee member for the Peace Officer Standards and Training Robert Presley Institute of Criminal Investigation Detective training symposium, Force Science Institute graduate, and Immediate Past President of the International Homicide Investigators Association. Belli holds a B.S. degree in criminal justice from California State University, Sacramento, in addition to Robert Presley Institute of Criminal Investigations certificates in Homicide and Narcotics investigations.

TIERRA BRADFORD (she/her/hers) is the senior program manager for the Justice team at The Leadership Conference on Civil and Human Rights. She works on a broad range of justice issues with specialized interests in pretrial, police accountability, and community safety. Prior to her current role with The Leadership Conference, she gained experience working on local, state, and national issues at the ACLU of Pennsylvania, Common Cause Maryland and Common Cause National. Bradford has a B.A. in psychology from Hampton University and a J.D. from the University of Pittsburgh School of Law.

REBECCA BROWN (she/her/hers) is founder of Maat Strategies. She joins the Quattrone Center after founding Maat Strategies, a consultancy that advises social justice organizations engaged in criminal legal reform. Prior to founding Maat Strategies, Brown worked at the Innocence Project—which is nationally recognized as one of the most transformative criminal legal reform organizations in the nation—for 18 years, helping to build and then lead its policy department, directing its federal and state policy agenda. During her tenure, the Innocence Project successfully lobbied the passage of more than 200 criminal legal reform laws. Brown has presented at judicial and legal trainings, diverse criminal justice, and academic conferences, and has been sought out as a subject matter expert by *The New York Times*, BBC News, ABC News, Slate, NBC News, CBS News, BNC News, Politico, NPR, and the *American Bar Association Journal*. Most recently, she appeared on a special episode of Meet the Press regarding police accountability.

JOHN M. BUTLER (he/him/his) is the president of the International Society for Forensic Genetics. His research, first conducted at the Federal Bureau of Investigation's Laboratory and now at the National Institute of Standards and Technology (NIST), pioneered the methods used today worldwide for

DNA testing in criminal casework, paternity investigations, and many DNA ancestry assessments. Butler has written six books on forensic DNA analysis and is a NIST fellow and special assistant to the director for forensic science. He has been honored in multiple White House ceremonies for his work in advancing DNA testing and has received the Gold Medal and Silver Medal from the U.S. Department of Commerce, the Scientific Prize of the International Society for Forensic Genetics, the Paul L. Kirk Award from the American Academy of Forensic Sciences, and the Magnus Mukoro Award for Integrity in Forensic Science from the NYC Legal Aid Society. Butler previously served as the vice-chair of the National Commission on Forensic Science. He holds a Ph.D. in analytical chemistry from the University of Virginia and is the most cited U.S. author in forensic science.

LEIGH CLARK (she/her/hers) is deputy director of forensic services at the Florida Department of Law Enforcement (FDLE). She discovered forensic science while teaching and working in police dispatch. Clark's forensic biology career commenced with the majority of her tenure at the FDLE, where she served as DNA technical leader for more than a decade and became deputy director of forensic services. She assists in direction of 10 disciplines across six regional laboratories and the state DNA database, and she oversees the statewide rape kit tracking system. Clark has provided programmatic and management support for automated workflows, familial searching, sexual assault kit testing, probabilistic genotyping, and forensic investigative genetic genealogy (FIGG). Presently, she helps monitor FDLE lab capability and capacity; assists in solicitation and management of grants and budgets; and liaises with external stakeholders. An original member of FDLE's team, she continues working in FIGG, through the National Technology Validation and Implementation Collaborative, and as an advisor to the Investigative Genetic Genealogy Accreditation Board. Clark is a member of the American Society of Crime Laboratory Directors, an active accrediting body technical assessor, and has presented throughout the United States and abroad. She completed her B.A. at University of Missouri (St. Louis), attended graduate school at Florida State, and completed her M.S. at University of Florida.

CLAIRE GLYNN (she/her/hers) is a professor of forensic science at the University of New Haven, Connecticut. She is also the executive director of the Henry C. Lee Institute of Forensic Science. Glynn's previously was employed as a forensic scientist at LGC Forensics (now called Eurofins) in Oxfordshire, United Kingdom. At the University of New Haven, she teaches courses and conducts extensive research focused on forensic biology, forensic DNA analysis, and forensic investigative genetic genealogy (FIGG).

APPENDIX B

Glynn is the founding director of the online Graduate Certificate in Forensic Investigative Genetic Genealogy (FIGG) at the University of New Haven, which is the first program of its kind in the world. She actively consults and provides subject matter expertise on FIGG and Forensic Science to law enforcement agencies in the United States and internationally.

RAFAELA GRANJA (she/her/hers) is a researcher at Communication and Society Research Centre at the University of Minho, Portugal. She is currently the principal investigator of the research project: E-MONITORING, Electronic Monitoring in the Criminal Justice System: Projected Futures and Lived Experiences (ref. 2023.00030.RESTART), funded by the Portuguese Foundation for Science and Technology. Granja's research interests lie at the intersection of sociology of crime and justice and social studies of science and technology and deal with the technological surveillance of criminalized populations at different stages of the criminal justice system, namely: criminal investigations, electronic monitoring and imprisonment. Her most recent publications include the books *Genetic Surveillance and Crime Control* (Routledge, 2022), *Modes of Bio-Bordering: The Hidden (Dis)Integration of Europe* (Palgrave, 2021), *Forensic Genetics in the Governance of Crime* (Palgrave, 2020). Granja holds a Ph.D. in sociology from the Institute of Social Sciences, University of Minho.

CHRISTI GUERRINI (she/her/hers) is assistant professor in the Center for Medical Ethics and Health Policy at Baylor College of Medicine and director of the Health Policy Pathway. She conducts research on the ethical, legal, and social implications of biomedical research and technologies, with a focus on genetics and genomics. Guerrini has served as principal investigator or co-investigator of National Institutes of Health–funded studies on investigative genetic genealogy (IGG), citizen science, and genomic data sharing. She has published on these and other topics in traditional law reviews and scientific journals, including *Science* and *Nature Biotechnology*. Related to IGG, Guerrini has served on the Investigative Genetic Genealogy Working Group of the Scientific Working Group on DNA Analysis Methods; the Policy and Procedure Subcommittee of the National Technology Validation and Implementation Collaborative Forensic Investigative Genetic Genealogy Technical Validation Working Group; and the Advisory Board of the Investigative Genetic Genealogy Accreditation Board. Prior to joining Baylor College of Medicine, she practiced law in Chicago and Houston. Guerrini received a B.A. from the University of Virginia, an M.P.H. from the University of Texas Health Science Center at Houston, and a J.D. from Harvard Law School.

DAN KATZ (he/him/his) is director with the Maryland State Police's Forensic Sciences Division. Previously, he served both as deputy director and forensic biology section manager with Maryland State Police's Forensic Sciences Division. Prior to coming to the Maryland State Police, Katz worked at the Delaware Office of the Chief Medical Examiner where he was the DNA unit manager and DNA technical leader. He started his forensic career at the Armed Forces DNA Identification Laboratory where he started as a technician and then as an analyst, in both the Mitochondrial DNA and Nuclear DNA sections. Katz is a member of the American Society of Crime Laboratory Directors, the Maryland Forensic Laboratory Advisory Committee, and a member of the Maryland Sexual Assault Evidence Kit Policy and Funding Committee. He is a former president of the Mid-Atlantic Association of Forensic Scientists, a fellow of the American Academy of Forensic Sciences, a past commissioner on the Forensic Science Education Program Accreditation Commission, and a founding member of the National Association of Forensic Science Boards. Katz received a B.S. in biotechnology from the University of Delaware, a M.F.S. in forensic science at the George Washington University, a certificate in forensic laboratory management from the University of California at Davis, and is certified by the American Board of Criminalistics as a diplomate in comprehensive criminalistics.

JENNIFER LYNCH (she/her/hers) is the general counsel at the Electronic Frontier Foundation (EFF), a nonprofit dedicated to the protection of privacy and civil liberties in new technologies. She has led EFF's legal work challenging government abuse of search and seizure technologies through litigation in state and federal courts, including the U.S. Supreme Court and founded EFF's Street Level Surveillance Project, which informs advocates, defense attorneys, and decisionmakers about new police tools. Lynch has written influential white papers on forensic genetic genealogy searches, law enforcement use of facial recognition, and biometric data collection in immigrant communities. She has also published articles on forensic genetic genealogy searches with the National Association of Criminal Defense Lawyers and on suspicionless police searches of consumer data for the Hoover Institution. Lynch has been named by *The Daily Journal* to its list of top lawyers of the decade for her work "guarding privacy in an over-policed world." She speaks frequently on technologies like location tracking, biometrics, and AI, and has testified on facial recognition before committees in the Senate and House of Representatives. Lynch is regularly consulted as an expert on these subjects and others by major and technical news media.

DAPHNE MARTSCHENKO (she/her/hers) is an assistant professor at the Stanford Center for Biomedical Ethics. Her work advocates for and facilitates research efforts that promote the socially and ethically responsible conduct and communication of and public engagement with human genetics and genomics. Martschenko is currently co-writing a book (under contract with Princeton University Press) with Sam Trejo, a quantitative sociologist who uses genomic data in his research. The book, titled *The Acid We Inherit*, is an adversarial collaboration that delves into the debates and controversies surrounding research connecting DNA to social and behavioral outcomes.

JEANNA MATTHEWS (she/her/hers) is a professor of computer science at Clarkson University. She is a founding chair of the Association for Computing Machinery's (ACM's) Technology Policy Subcommittee on Artificial Intelligence and Algorithmic Accountability, a vice-chair of Institute of Electrical and Electronics Engineers—USA AI Policy Committee, and a member of the ACM Technology Policy Committee. Matthews has been a faculty fellow at National Institute of Standards and Technology, a member of the National Science Foundation's Computer and Information Science and Engineering Advisory Council, an affiliate at Data and Society, a member of the ACM Council, a chair of the ACM Special Interest Group Governing Board, the chair of the ACM Special Interest Group on Operating Systems, chair of the Viewpoints section of the *Communications of the ACM* magazine, an ACM distinguished speaker, and a Fulbright Scholar. She has published work in a broad range of systems topics from virtualization and cloud computing. Matthews received a Brown Institute Magic Grant to research differences in DNA software programs used in the criminal justice system. She received a B.A. in Spanish from the State University of New York at Potsdam, a B.S. in mathematics and computer science from Ohio State University, and a Ph.D. in computer science from the University of California at Berkeley.

CAROLE McCARTNEY (she/her/hers) is professor of law and criminal justice at the University of Leicester. She is currently a commissioner on the All Party Parliamentary Group on Miscarriages of Justice's Westminster Commission on Forensic Science. Previously at Northumbria University, where she established the Science and Justice Research Interest Group, McCartney has been researching issues around criminal evidence and forensic science for more than twenty years, and has written on miscarriages of justice, DNA and biometrics, forensic science, and criminal justice more widely.

DENNIS McNEVIN (he/him/his) is professor of forensic genetics at the University of Technology Sydney. His teaching and research are focused on the use of technology to enhance the value of DNA in forensic investigations. McNevin has previously worked for the Australian Federal Police and has provided DNA analysis services to multiple jurisdictions in Australia.

He has more than one hundred publications in journals including *Nature Communications*, *Journal of Biological Chemistry*, *Forensic Science International*, *Forensic Science International Genetics*, *International Journal of Legal Medicine*, *Forensic Science Medicine and Pathology*, and *Science and Justice*.

ERIN MURPHY (she/her/hers) is Norman Dorsen professor of civil liberties at New York University School of Law. She is an internationally recognized expert in forensic DNA typing, and the author of *Inside the Cell: The Dark Side of Forensic DNA* (2015) and co-editor of the *Modern Scientific Evidence: The Law and Science of Expert Testimony*. Murphy served as the associate reporter for the American Law Institute's successful revision of Article 213 (Sexual Assault and Related Offenses) of the Model Penal Code and senior policy advisor for criminal justice at the White House Domestic Policy Council. Her research focuses on the criminal legal system, with a particular focus on questions related to forensic science, policing and new technologies, sexual assault, and drug policy. Murphy has translated her scholarly writing for more popular audiences by publishing in *Science*, *Scientific American*, *New Scientist*, *New York Times*, *Washington Post*, *San Francisco Chronicle*, *USA Today*, *Slate*, *The Atlantic*, and *New Republic*, and has offered commentary for numerous media outlets, including NPR, PBS, CNN, Fox, MSNBC, and NBC Nightly News. A proud recipient of the Podell Distinguished Teaching Award, her course offerings include criminal law and procedure, evidence, forensic evidence, and professional responsibility in the criminal context.

MARK POOLEY (he/him/his) is the director, investigative support (American Indian/Alaska Native) for The University of North Texas Health Science Center's Center for Human Identification (CHI). In this position, he assists law enforcement agencies seeking to provide answers for missing and unidentified persons, their families, and the community, with a focus on American Indian/Alaska Native communities. Pooley joined CHI a few years after he retired as a sergeant from the Tempe Police Department in Arizona. During his tenure in law enforcement, he held several detective positions in Robbery, the Joint Terrorism Task Force, Homicide/Missing Persons and as a supervisor in the Professional Standard's Bureau. Pooley, as a Navajo and Hopi, worked a tribal prosecutor for the Salt River Pima-Maricopa Indian Community where he dealt with criminal and civil issues within the tribal court. He started a 501(c)(3) nonprofit called Native Search Solutions, which has the mission of finding Missing & Murdered Indigenous People on and off the reservation(s) by using technology and other resources. Pooley was the inaugural tribal fellow for the National Center for Missing & Exploited Children, where he supported outreach to Native, Indigenous, and tribal communities. He holds a B.A. in political science from Brigham Young University and an M.Ed. in counseling-human relations from Northern Arizona University.

NORAH RUDIN (she/her/hers) is a member of the California Association of Criminalists, a fellow of the American Academy of Forensic Sciences, and has been a diplomate of the American Board of Criminalistics. After completing a post-doctoral fellowship at Lawrence Berkeley Laboratory, she served three years as a full-time consultant/technical leader for the California Department of Justice DNA Laboratory and has also served as consulting technical leader for the Idaho Department of Law Enforcement DNA Laboratory, the San Francisco Crime Laboratory DNA Section, and the San Diego County Sheriff's Department DNA Laboratory. Rudin has co-authored *An Introduction to DNA Forensic Analysis* and *Principles and Practice of Criminalistics: The Profession of Forensic Science*. She is also the author of the *Dictionary of Modern Biology*. Rudin has taught a variety of general forensic and forensic DNA courses for the University of California at Berkeley and online. She is frequently invited to speak at various legal symposia and forensic conferences. Rudin has served a gubernatorial appointment to the Virginia Department of Forensic Science Scientific Advisory Committee and has been a co-chair of the Constitution Project Committee on DNA Collection. She was part of the group that developed Lab Retriever, an early probabilistic genotyping software tool. Rudin has co-authored peer-reviewed articles on the topic of probabilistic genotyping and provided training to both scientists and attorneys on the subject. She remains active as an independent consultant and expert witness in forensic DNA. Rudin holds a B.A. from Pomona College and a Ph.D. from Brandeis University.

JEREMY TRIPLETT (he/him/his) is the director of the Kentucky State Police Central Forensic Laboratory where he oversees the day-to-day operations of the full service, ISO 17025 accredited laboratory. He has experience in forensic science with a background in seized drugs analysis and has testified in local, state, and federal courts. Triplett is a past-president of the American Society of Crime Laboratory Directors, an organization of crime laboratory directors and managers dedicated to providing excellence in forensic science through leadership and innovation. He also served as chairman of the Forensic Science Standards Board of the National Institute of Standards and Technology's Organization of Scientific Area Committees. Triplett is a member of the American Academy of Forensic Sciences, the International Association of Chiefs of Police forensic committee, the strategic advisory board for the Center for Statistics and Applications in Forensic Science and serves as technical assessor in seized drugs for the American

National Standards Institute's National Accreditation Board, where he has participated in assessments of forensic science laboratories inside and outside of the United States. He received a B.S. in chemistry from the University of Kentucky and an M.S. in pharmacy from the University of Florida.

KRYSTAL TSOSIE (she/her/hers) is an assistant professor at Arizona State University in the School of Life Sciences. As Diné within the Navajo Nation, she co-founded the first U.S. Indigenous-led biobank, a 501(c)(3) nonprofit research institution called the Native BioData Consortium. Tsosie's research centers on ethical engagement with Indigenous communities in precision health and genomic medicine. Her areas include genetic epidemiology, bioethics, public health, and community research approaches. Tsosie previously patented a combined targeted ultrasound imaging and chemotherapeutic drug delivery device for treating early metastases in cancer. She is currently on the Board of Directors for the American Society of Human Genetics, and on the ethics committee of the American Society for Cell and Gene Therapies. Tsosie has a M.A. in bioethics for studying genetic controversies in Indigenous communities, a M.P.H. in genetic epidemiology for studying gene variation related to hypertension and uterine fibroids, and a Ph.D. in genomics and health disparities. She recently served on the National Academies of Sciences, Engineering, and Medicine's consensus study committee, Creating a Framework for Emerging Science, Technology, and Innovation in Health and Medicine and on the National Academies' planning committee, Engaging Scientists in Central Asia on Data Governance Principles for Life Science Data.

RAYMOND VALERIO (he/him/his) is an assistant district attorney in New York City and is the director of forensic sciences at the Queens County District Attorney's Office, where he oversees all forensic science-based prosecutions. He is a member of the Organization of Scientific Area Committees Firearm and Toolmark Subcommittee, the Firearm Toolmark and Friction Ridge American Standards Consensus Bodies of the American Academy of Forensic Sciences, the National District Attorneys Association Forensic Science Working Group, and serves on the Strategic Advisory Board for the Center for Statistics and Applications in Forensic Evidence. Valerio received the Thomas E. Dewey Medal from the New York City Bar Association for his accomplishments in forensic science as a prosecutor. *Scientific American* published his opinion editorial "Firearm Forensics Has Proven Reliable in the Courtroom. And in the Lab" and *WIRE Interdisciplinary Journal*, a peer-reviewed journal, published Valerio's article titled "Likelihood Ratios for Lawyers...I Didn't Go to Law School for This."

SUSAN WALSH (she/her/hers) is an associate professor of biology at Indiana University Indianapolis where her laboratory focuses on understanding the genetics of human physical appearance, from pigment to facial structure, and its prediction from DNA. She was a research assistant at the University of Sydney (Australia) and a postdoctoral research associate in anthropology at Yale University. Walsh has published more than 40 peer-reviewed articles in the last decade spanning the fields of genetics, forensics and bioinformatics. Her research has been funded by National Institute of Justice, Department of Defense, and National Institutes of Health. Walsh received her B.S. in biochemistry from University College Cork (Ireland), a M.S. in DNA profiling from the University of Central Lancashire (United Kingdom), and a Ph.D. in forensic genetics from Erasmus University (the Netherlands).

REBECCA WEXLER (she/her/hers) is an assistant professor of law at University of California, Berkeley School of Law, and faculty co-director of the Berkeley Center for Law and Technology. Her teaching and research focus on data, technology, and secrecy in the criminal legal system. Wexler's scholarship has appeared or is forthcoming in the *Harvard Law Review, Stanford Law Review, Yale Law Journal Forum, New York University Law Review, University of California, Los Angeles Law Review, Texas Law Review, Vanderbilt Law Review,* and *Berkeley Technology Law Journal*, as well as in peer-reviewed computer science publications.

RAY WICKENHAUSER (he/him/his) is the director for the New York State Police Crime Laboratory System, headquartered in Albany, New York. He is a past president of the American Society of Crime Laboratory Directors and a Briggs J. White Award recipient. Wickenhauser is a member of the National Technology Validation and Implementation Steering Committee, the chair of the Forensic Investigative Genetic Genealogy Policy and Procedures Committee, and co-chair of the Rapid DNA Committee. He was formerly the chair of the Forensic Science Standards Board for the Organization of Scientific Area Committees for Forensic Science and an invited guest to the Scientific Working Group on DNA Analysis. Wickenhauser was formerly an auditor and lead DNA auditor with the International Organization for Standardization. He has more than 40 years of experience working in the field of forensic science. Wickenhauser's areas of expertise include crime lab administration, quality management, conflict resolution, forensic DNA and mixture interpretation, serology, hair and fiber trace evidence, physical matching and comparison, glass fracture analysis, forensic grain comparison and forensic investigative genetic genealogy. He holds a bachelor of science honors degree from the University of Regine, Canada, a master of business administration degree from the University of Louisiana at Lafayette, Louisiana and a doctoral degree from the Albany Medical College.

MATTHIAS WIENROTH (he/him/his) is assistant professor at the Northumbria University Centre for Crime and Policing. His work attends to the overall question of how bioscientific knowledge and biotechnologies can contribute to a "good society." More specifically, Wienroth studies social, ethical, operational, and oversight aspects of biometrics data and technologies in justice, security, and health contexts, analyzing how these data and technologies contribute to identity and identification—i.e., the (un-)knowing of human beings (e.g., for forensic, surveillance, and health purposes)—and the (re-)production of social orders. Most recently, his work has focused on the ethics of forensic genetics and of biometric data categorization, developing the RULE framework (reliability, utility, legitimacy) and co-developing a professional integrity framework for good ethical self-governance and external oversight of these fields.

LUCAS ZARWELL (he/him/his) is the office director for the Office of Investigative and Forensic Sciences at the National Institute of Justice (NIJ). He leads a team of dedicated forensic scientists who work to facilitate research and implement new technologies nationwide. Prior to this position, Zarwell served as chief toxicologist for the District of Columbia (DC) Chief Medical Examiner, DC Pre-Trial Services Forensic Drug Testing Laboratory, and the Armed Forces Institute of Pathology. He currently co-chairs the Office of Justice Programs/Department of Health and Human Services Federal Interagency Medicolegal Death Investigation Working Group, which is hosted by NIJ. Zarwell holds a M.S. in forensic science from George Washington University and maintains his certification from the American Board of Forensic Toxicology.

MARTIN ZIEGER (he/him/his) is a research group leader and forensic expert at the Institute of Forensic Medicine, University of Bern, Switzerland. His research activities cover a diverse range of topics, including population genetics, DNA sampling strategies, and DNA transfer and persistence. Zieger's particular interest lies in the legal regulation of forensic genetics. He was involved as an expert at various stages in the recent revision of the Swiss DNA Profiles Act. Zieger is a member of the Forensic Databases Advisory Board of the International Society for Forensic Genetics and a member of the Swiss Federal Commission for Human Genetic Testing. He holds a M.Law, a Ph.D. in biochemistry, and the specialist title of forensic geneticist from the Swiss Society of Forensic Medicine.

Appendix C

Bibliography for Workshop Speaker Presentations

Aldhous, P. (2019, May 14). The arrest of a teen on an assault charge has sparked new privacy fears about DNA sleuthing. *Buzzfeed News.* https://www.buzzfeednews.com/article/peteraldhous/genetic-genealogy-parabon-gedmatch-assault

Amankwaa, A., & McCartney, C. (2018). The UK National DNA Database: Implementation of the Protection of Freedoms Act 2012. *Forensic Science International, 284,* 117–128.

———. (2019). The effectiveness of the UK National DNA Database. *Forensic Science International: Synergy, 1,* 45–55. https://doi.org/10.1016/j.fsisyn.2019.03.004

———. (2020). Gaughran vs the UK and public acceptability of forensic biometrics retention. *Science and Justice, 60*(3), 204–205. https://doi.org/10.1016/j.scijus.2020.04.001

———. (2021). The effectiveness of the current use of forensic DNA in criminal investigations in England & Wales. *WIREs Forensic Science,* e1414. https://doi.org/10.1002/wfs2.1414

———. (2022). Evaluating forensic DNA databases. In V. Toom, M. Wienroth, & A. M'charek (Eds)., *Law, practice and politics of forensic DNA profiling.* Routledge.

Bai, S., Li, M. Z., Wan, Y. Y., Hu, X. C., Liu, Y. X., Tong, X. H., Guo, T. H., Zong, L., Liu, R., Zhao, Y. Q., Xiang, P., Xu, B., & Jiang, X. H. (2024). Association between MTHFR c.677C>T variant and erectile dysfunction among males attending fertility clinic. *Asian Journal of Andrology, 26*(1), 41–45. https://doi.org/10.4103/aja202335

Bright, J. A., Jones Dukes, M., Pugh, S. N., Evett, I. W., & Buckleton, J. S. (2019). Applying calibration to *LR*s produced by a DNA interpretation software. *Australian Journal of Forensic Sciences, 53*(2), 147–153. https://doi.org/10.1080/00450618.2019.1682668

Bright, J. A., Richards, R., Kruijver, M., Kelly, H., McGovern, C., Magee, A., McWhorter, A., Ciecko, A., Peck, B., Baumgartner, C., Buettner, C., McWilliams, S., McKenna, C., Gallacher, C., Mallinder, B., Wright, D., Johnson, D., Catella, D., Lien, E., O'Connor, C., … Buckleton, J. S. (2018). Internal validation of STRmix™—A multi laboratory response to PCAST. *Forensic Science International: Genetics, 34,* 11–24. https://doi.org/10.1016/j.fsigen.2018.01.003

Buckleton, J. S., Kruijver, M., Curran, J., & Bright, J. (2020). *Calibration of STRmix LRs following the method of Hannig et al.* Institute of Environmental Science and Research. https://doi.org/10.26091/ESRNZ.12324011.v1

Butler, J. M., Iyer, H., Press, R., Taylor, M. K., Vallone, P. M., & Willis, S. (2021). *DNA mixture interpretation: A NIST scientific foundation review*. National Institute of Standards and Technology. https://nvlpubs.nist.gov/nistpubs/ir/2021/NIST.IR.8351-draft.pdf

Caldero, M., Dailey, J., & Withrow, B. (2018). *Police ethics: The corruption of noble cause*. Routledge. https://doi.org/10.4324/9781315162591

CBC News. (2022, October 6). *Edmonton police issue apology for controversial use of DNA phenotyping*. https://www.cbc.ca/news/canada/edmonton/edmonton-police-issue-apology-for-controversial-use-of-dna-phenotyping-1.6608457

Cha, A. E. (2019). There's no "gay gene," but genetics are linked to same-sex behavior, new study says. *The Washington Post*, August 29. https://www.washingtonpost.com/health/2019/08/29/theres-no-gay-gene-genetics-are-linked-same-sex-behavior-new-study-says

Chomsky, A. (2018, November 29). DNA tests make Native Americans strangers in their own land. *The Nation*. https://www.thenation.com/article/archive/dna-tests-elizabeth-warren-native-american-race-science/

Collins, E., Learner, N., & Gutman, J. (2008). *Report on patient privacy: Practical news and strategies for complying with HIPPA Rules*. Atlantic Information Services, Inc. https://assets.hcca-info.org/Portals/0/PDFs/Resources/Rpt_Privacy/2008/rpp0508.pdf

Curtis, C., Hereward, J., Mangelsdorf, M., Hussey, K., & Devereux, J. (2019). Protecting trust in medical genetics in the new era of forensics. *Genetics in Medicine*, 21(7), 1483–1485.

Dahlquist, J., Robinson, J. O., Daoud, A., Bash Brooks, W., McGuire, A. L., Guerrini, C. J., & Fullerton, S. M. (In press). Public perspectives on investigative genetic genealogy: Findings from a national focus group study. *AJOB Empirical Bioethics*. https://doi.org/10.1080/23294515.2024.2336904

de Groot, N. F. (2023). Commercial genetic information and criminal investigations: The case for social privacy. *Big Data & Society*. https://doi.org/10.1177/20539517231211695

Devlin, H. (2015). Risk of sex offending linked to genetic factors, study finds. *The Guardian*, April 9. https://www.theguardian.com/science/2015/apr/09/risk-of-sex-offending-linked-to-genetic-factors-study-finds

Dowdeswell, T. L. (2022). Forensic genetic genealogy: A profile of cases solved. *Forensic Science International: Genetics*, 58, 102679.

Evans, J. (2018, May 6). Personal privacy vs. public security. *Tech Crunch*. https://techcrunch.com/2018/05/06/personal-privacy-vs-public-security-fight/?guccounter=1

Federal Act on the Use of DNA Profiles in Criminal Proceedings and for Identifying Unidentified or Missing Persons (DNA Profiles Act). (2003). Swiss Confederation. https://www.fedlex.admin.ch/eli/cc/2004/811/en

Federal Bureau of Investigation. (2019). *Expanded homicide data table 6, murder, race, sex and ethnicity of offender, 2019 [Single victim/single offender]*. https://ucr.fbi.gov/crime-in-the-u.s/2019/crime-in-the-u.s.-2019/tables/expanded-homicide-data-table-6.xls

Frosh, D. (2024). Colorado's star DNA Analyst intentionally manipulated data, investigation finds. *The Wall Street Journal*, March 8. https://www.wsj.com/us-news/colorados-star-dna-analyst-intentionally-manipulated-data-investigation-finds-eff028ac

Gabrielson, R. (2017, April 14). Another startling verdict for forensic science. *ProPublica*. https://www.propublica.org/article/another-startling-verdict-for-forensic-science-1

Ganna, A., Verweij, K. J. H., Nivard, M. G., Maier, R., Wedow, R., Busch, A. S., Abdellaoui, A., Guo, S., Sathirapongsasuti, J. F., Lichtenstein, P., Lundström, S., Långström, N., Auton, A., Harris, K. M., Beecham, G. W., Martin, E. R., Sanders, A. R., B. Perry, J. R., Neale, B. M., & Zietsch, B. P. (2019). Large-scale GWAS reveals insights into the genetic architecture of same-sex sexual behavior. *Science*, 365(6456). https://doi.org/10.1126/science.aat7693

Gibson, C. (2022, October 6). Edmonton police apologize after concerns raised over release of DNA phenotyping composite sketch. *Global News*. https://globalnews.ca/news/9181617/edmonton-police-apology-dna-phenotyping-composite-sketch

Glynn, C. L. (2022). Bridging disciplines to form a new one: The emergency of forensic genetic genealogy. *Genes, 13*, 1381.

Government Accountability Office. (2019). *DNA evidence: DOJ should improve performance measurement and properly design controls for nationwide grant program.* https://www.gao.gov/products/gao-19-216

Granja, R. (2020). Long-range familial searches in recreational DNA databases: Expansion of affected populations, the participatory turn, and the co-production of biovalue. *New Genetics and Society, 40*(3), 331–352. https://doi.org/10.1080/14636778.2020.1853515

———. (2023). Citizen science at the roots and as the future of forensic genetic genealogy. *International Journal of Police Science & Management.* https://doi.org/10.1177/14613557231164901

Greytak, E. M., Moore, C., & Armentrout, S. L. (2019). Genetic genealogy for cold case and active investigations. *Forensic Science International 299*, 103–113.

Guerrini, C. J., Robinson, J. O., Petersen, D., & McGuire, A. L. (2018). Should police have access to genetic genealogy databases? Capturing the Golden State Killer and other criminals using a controversial new forensic technique. *PLoS Biology, 16*(10), e2006906.

Guerrini, C. J., Wickenheiser, R. A., Bettinger, B., McGuire, A. L., & Fullerton, S. M. (2021). Four misconceptions about investigative genetic genealogy. *Journal of Law and the Biosciences, 8*(1). https://doi.org/10.1093/jlb/lsab001

Guerrini, C. J., Bash Brooks, W., Robinson, J. O., Fullerton, S. M., Zoorob, E., & McGuire, A. L. (2024). IGG in the trenches: Results of an in-depth interview study on the practice, politics, and future of investigative genetic genealogy. *Forensic Science International, 356*, 111946.

Gurney, D., Press. M., Moore, C., Rolnick, C. I., Hochreiter, A., & Bossert, B. L. (2022). The need for standards and certification for investigative genetic genealogy, and a notice of action. *Forensic Science International, 341*, 111495.

Haag, M. (2019, February 4). FamilyTreeDNA admits to sharing genetic data with F.B.I. *The New York Times.* https://www.nytimes.com/2019/02/04/business/family-tree-dna-fbi.html

Hannig, J., Riman, S., Iyer, H., & Vallone, P. M. (2019). Are reported likelihood ratios well calibrated? *Forensic Science International: Genetics, 7*(1), 572–574. https://doi.org/10.1016/j.fsigss.2019.10.094

Harkins, G. (2019, December 27). Pentagon leaders tell troops to stop using mail-in genealogy DNA kits. *Military.com.* https://www.military.com/daily-news/2019/12/27/pentagon-leaders-tell-troops-stop-using-mail-genealogy-dna-kits.html

Haskell v. Harris, 669 F.3d 1049 (9th Cir. 2012). https://law.justia.com/cases/federal/appellate-courts/ca9/10-15152/10-15152-2014-03-20.html

Haywood, P. (2018, November 23). "Warrior gene" appeal to be heard by New Mexico Supreme Court. *Santa Fe New Mexican.* https://www.santafenewmexican.com/news/local_news/warrior-gene-appeal-to-be-heard-by-new-mexico-supreme-court/article_b34b0e52-da69-5a9a-a6b8-d8d52ea4cb3d.html

Hill, K., & Murphy, H. (2019, November 5). Your DNA profile is private? A Florida judge just said otherwise. *The New York Times.* https://www.nytimes.com/2019/11/05/business/dna-database-search-warrant.html

Investigative Genetic Genealogy. (2023). *Professional standards and accreditation requirements.* https://www.iggab.org/uploads/1/4/2/9/142901820/s001_investigative_genetic_genealogy_professional_standards_and_accreditation_requirements_publication.pdf

Justice in Forensic Algorithms Act, H. R. 7394, 118th Cong. (2024). https://www.congress.gov/bill/118th-congress/house-bill/7394/text

Lipphardt, A. (2020). The invention of the Phantom of Heilbronn. *Journal for European Ethnology and Cultural Analysis, 4*(1). https://elibrary.utb.de/doi/abs/10.31244/jeeca.2019.01.03

McCartney, C., Granja, R., & Topfer, E. (2023). Biometric forensic identity databases: Precariously balanced or faulty scales? In A. Roberts, J. Purshouse, & J. Bosland (Eds.), *Privacy, technology & the criminal process*. Routledge.

McShane, L., & Parascandola, R. (2021, December 9). NYPD still using controversial DNA lab for investigations. *New York Daily News*. https://www.nydailynews.com/2021/12/09/nypd-still-using-controversial-dna-lab-for-investigations-more-than-a-year-after-city-hall-said-ties-were-cut

Medina, E. (2022, September 13). Woman sues San Francisco over arrest based on DNA from her rape kit. *The New York Times*. https://www.nytimes.com/2022/09/13/us/rape-kit-dna-san-francisco.html

Mehotra, D. (2024, January 22). Cops used DNA to predict a suspect's face—And tried to run facial recognition on it. *WIRED*. https://www.wired.com/story/parabon-nanolabs-dna-face-models-police-facial-recognition

Mentis, A., Dardiotis, E., Katsouni, E., & Chrousos, G. P. (2021). From warrior genes to translational solutions: Novel insights into monoamine oxidases (MAOs) and aggression. *Translational Psychiatry*, *11*(1), 1–11. https://doi.org/10.1038/s41398-021-01257-2

Modarressy-Tehrani, C. (2019). A DNA test revealed this man is 4% Black. Now he wants to abolish affirmative action. *HuffPost*. https://www.huffpost.com/entry/dna-test-affirmative-action_n_5d824762e4b0957256afa986

Morgan, R. E. (2017). *Race and Hispanic origin of victims and offenders* (Special Report No. 2012-15, NCJ 250747). U.S. Department of Justice, Office of Justice Programs, Bureau of Justice Statistics. https://bjs.ojp.gov/content/pub/pdf/rhovo1215.pdf

Mullin, E. (2023, November 8). New Jersey keeps newborn DNA for 23 years. Parents are suing. *WIRED*. https://www.wired.com/story/new-jersey-keeps-newborn-dna-for-23-years-parents-are-suing

Murphy, E. (2018). Law and policy oversight of familial searches in recreational genealogy databases. *Forensic Science International*, *292*, e5–e9. https://doi.org/10.1016/j.forsciint.2018.08.027

Murrell, D. (2019, December 9). Some Philly-area police departments have used DNA to create CGI sketches of suspects. *Philadelphia Magazine*. https://www.phillymag.com/news/2019/12/09/dna-phenotyping

National Academies of Sciences, Engineering, and Medicine. (2023). *Using population descriptors in genetics and genomics research: A new framework for an evolving field*. National Academies Press. https://doi.org/10.17226/26902

National Institute on Drug Abuse. (2023). *New NIH study reveals shared genetic markers underlying substance use disorders*. https://nida.nih.gov/news-events/news-releases/2023/03/new-nih-study-reveals-shared-genetic-markers-underlying-substance-use-disorders

Newman, M. (2019, October 7). Rabbinate DNA tests seek Jewishness in the blood, become a bone of contention. *The Times of Israel*. https://www.timesofisrael.com/rabbinate-dna-tests-seek-jewishness-in-the-blood-become-a-bone-of-contention

Nooruddin, M., Scherr, C., Friedman, P., Subrahmanyam, R., Banagan, J., Moreno, D., Sathyanarayanan, M., Nutescu, E., Jeyaram, T., Harris, M., Zhang, H., Rodriguez, A., Shaazuddin, M., Perera, M., & Tuck, M. (2020). Why African Americans say "No." *Ethnicity & Disease*, *159*. https://doi.org/48668434

Orrù, E., Porcedda, M. G., & Weydner-Volkmann, S. (Eds.). (2017). *Rethinking surveillance and control. Beyond the 'security vs. privacy' debate*. Nomos.

Padawer, R. (2018, November 19). Sigrid Johnson was Black. A DNA test said she wasn't. *The New York Times*. https://www.nytimes.com/2018/11/19/magazine/dna-test-black-family.html

Panofsky, A., Dasgupta, K., & Iturriaga, N. (2021). How White nationalists mobilize genetics: From genetic ancestry and human biodiversity to counterscience and metapolitics. *American Journal of Physical Anthropology*, *175*(2), 387–398. https://doi.org/10.1002/ajpa.24150

Parikh, R., Salowe, R., Mccoskey, M., Pan, W., Sankar, P., Miller-Ellis, E., Addis, V., Lehman, A., & Maguire, M. (2019). Factors associated with participation by African Americans in a study of the genetics of glaucoma. *Ethnicity & Health*, 24(6), 694. https://doi.org/10.1080/13557858.2017.1346189

Patel, V. (2022, June 10). Idaho city to pay $11.7 Million to man wrongfully convicted in 1996 killing. *New York Times*. https://www.nytimes.com/2022/06/10/us/idaho-falls-christopher-tapp-settlement.html

President's Council of Advisors on Science and Technology. (2016). *Forensic science in criminal courts: Ensuring scientific validity of feature-comparison methods.* Executive Office of the President. https://obamawhitehouse.archives.gov/sites/default/files/microsites/ostp/PCAST/pcast_forensic_science_report_final.pdf

Prince, E. R., Uhlmann, W. R., Suter, S. M., & Scherer, A. M. (2021). Genetic testing and insurance implications: Surveying the US general population about discrimination concerns and knowledge of the Genetic Information Nondiscrimination Act (GINA). *Risk Management and Insurance Review*, 24(4), 341. https://doi.org/10.1111/rmir.12195

Race and crime in the United States. (n.d.). *Wikipedia*. https://en.wikipedia.org/wiki/Race_and_crime_in_the_United_States

Rae-Venter, B. (2023). *I know who you are: How an amateur DNA sleuth unmasked the Golden State Killer.* Ballantine Books.

Ram, N. (2018). Incidental informants: Police can use genealogy databases to help identify criminal relatives—But should they? *Maryland State Bar Journal*, 51(3), 8–12.

Ram, N., Murphy, E. E., & Suter, S. M. (2021). Regulating forensic genetic genealogy. *Science*, 373(6562), 1444–1446. https://doi.org/10.1126/science.abj5724

Revision of the DNA Profiles Act. (2023, May 15). Swiss Federal Office of Police. https://www.fedpol.admin.ch/fedpol/en/home/sicherheit/personenidentifikation-neu/dna-und-codis/dna-profilgesetz.html

Scharff, D. P., Mathews, K. J., Jackson, P., Hoffsuemmer, J., Martin, E., & Edwards, D. (2010). More than Tuskegee: Understanding mistrust about research participation. *Journal of Health Care for the Poor and Underserved*, 21(3), 879. https://doi.org/10.1353/hpu.0.0323

Schuppe, J. (2020, February 22). "They lied to us": Mom says police deceived her to get her DNA and charge her son with murder. *NBC News*. https://www.nbcnews.com/news/us-news/they-lied-us-mom-says-police-deceived-her-get-her-n1140696

Simon, S. (2019, December 7). Uighurs and genetic surveillance in China. *National Public Radio*. https://www.npr.org/2019/12/07/785804791/uighurs-and-genetic-surveillance-in-china

Smith, J. (2023, August 18). People are getting DNA data from people who think they opted out. *The Intercept*. https://theintercept.com/2023/08/18/gedmatch-dna-police-forensic-genetic-genealogy

Taylor, D., Buckleton, J., & Evett, I. (2015). Testing likelihood ratios produced from complex DNA profiles. *Forensic Science International: Genetics*, 16, 165–171. https://doi.org/10.1016/j.fsigen.2015.01.008

Thomson, J., Clayton, T., Cleary, J., Gleeson, M., Kennett, D., Leonard, M., & Rutherford, D. (2020). An empirical investigation into the effectiveness of genetic genealogy to identify individuals in the UK. *Forensic Science International: Genetics*, 46, 102263.

Tillmar, A., Fagerholm, S. A., Staaf, J., Sjölund, P., & Ansell, R. (2021). Getting the conclusive lead with investigative genetic genealogy—A successful case study of a 16 year old double murder in Sweden. *Forensic Science International: Genetics*, 53, 102525.

Truman, J. L., & Langton, L. (2014). *Criminal victimization.* Bureau of Justice Statistics. https://www.bjs.gov/content/pub/pdf/cv14.pdf

Tvedebrink, T. (2022). Review of the forensic applicability of biostatistical methods for inferring ancestry from autosomal genetic markers. *Genes*, 13(1), 141. https://doi.org/10.3390/genes13010141

U.S. Department of Justice. (2019). *Interim policy on forensic genetic genealogical DNA analysis and searching.* https://www.justice.gov/olp/page/file/1204386/download

United States v. Amerson, 483 F.3d 73 (2d Cir. 2007).

United States v. Kriesel, 720 F.3d 1137 (9th Cir. 2013).

United States v. Mitchell, 652 F.3d 387 (3d Cir. 2011).

United States v. Weikert, 504 F.3d 1 (1st Cir. 2007).

Utah Public Safety Code § 53-10-403.7 (2023). Investigative genetic genealogy service. https://le.utah.gov/xcode/Title53/Chapter10/53-10-S403.7.html?v=C53-10-S403.7_2023050320230503

Verogen increases costs for law enforcement—Again. (2022, December 17). *The DNA Geek.* https://thednageek.com/verogen-increases-costs-for-law-enforcement-again

Waltes, R., Chiocchetti, A. G., & Freitag, C. M. (2016). The neurobiological basis of human aggression: A review on genetic and epigenetic mechanisms. *American Journal of Medical Genetics: Part B, Neuropsychiatric Genetics, 171*(5), 650–675. https://doi.org/10.1002/ajmg.b.32388

Whittaker, Z. (2021, February 10). Ancestry says it fought two police requests to search its DNA database. *Tech Crunch.* https://techcrunch.com/2021/02/10/ancestry-police-warrant-dna-database

Wickenheiser, R. A. (2019). Forensic genealogy, bioethics and the Golden State Killer case. *Forensic Science International: Synergy, 1,* 114.

Wickenheiser, R. A., Naugle, J., Hoey, B., Nowlin, R., Kumar, S. A., Kubinski, M., Glynn, C., Valerio, R., Allen, L., Stoiloff, S., Kochanski, J., Guerrini, C., & Schubert, A. M. (2023). National Technology Validation and Implementation Collaborative (NTVIC): Guidelines for establishing forensic investigative genetic genealogy (FIGG) programs. *Forensic Science International: Synergy, 7,* 100446. https://doi.org/10.1016/j.fsisyn.2023.100446

Wienroth, M. (2020). Value beyond scientific validity: Let's RULE (Reliability, Utility, LEgitimacy). *Journal of Responsible Innovation, 7*(Suppl 1), 92–103. https://doi.org/10.1080/23299460.2020.1835152

Wienroth, M., & Granja, R. (2024). Dissolving boundaries, fostering dependencies: The new forensic genetics assemblage. *Science, Technology & Human Values.* https://doi.org/10.1177/01622439241266055

Wienroth, M., & McCartney, C. (2024). "Noble cause casuistry" in forensic genetics. *Wiley Interdisciplinary Reviews: Forensic Science, 6*(1), e1502. https://doi.org/10.1002/wfs2.1502

Wienroth, M., Granja, R., Lipphardt, V., Nsiah Amoako, E., & McCartney, C. (2021). Ethics as lived practice: Anticipatory capacity and ethical decision-making in forensic genetics. *Genes, 12*(12), 1868. https://doi.org/10.3390/genes12121868

Wienroth, M., Amankwaa, A., & McCartney, C. (2022). Integrity, trustworthiness and effectiveness: An ethos for forensic genetics. *Genes, 13*(8), 1453. https://doi.org/10.3390/genes13081453

Worth, K. (2018, April 19). Framed for murder by his own DNA. *The Marshall Project.* https://www.themarshallproject.org/2018/04/19/framed-for-murder-by-his-own-dna

Zieger, M. (2022). Forensic DNA phenotyping in Europe: How far may it go? *Journal of Law and the Biosciences, 9*(2), lsac024. https://doi.org/10.1093/jlb/lsac024